THE BLOODY MARY BOOK

Reinventing a Classic Cocktail

By Ellen Brown

RUNNING PRESS

PHILADELPHIA

Design by Joshua McDonnell
Edited by Kristen Green Wiewora
Typography: Brandon, Bembo, and Harman
Food Stylist: Anna Hampton (back cover and interior)
Food Stylist: Mariana Velasquez (front cover)
Prop Stylist: Kristi Hunter

Running Press Book Publishers
2300 Chestnut Street
Philadelphia, PA 19103-4371

Visit us on the web!
www.offthemenublog.com

TABLE OF CONTENTS

Acknowledgments

While writing a book and developing recipes are solitary endeavors, transforming them into an exciting book certainly takes a village or two. My thanks go:

To Kristen Green Wiewora, editor extraordinaire, for appreciating that Bloody Mary variations really do need recipes, as well as yummy foods to serve with them.

To Joshua McDonnell, the talented designer at Running Press who created the dramatic look of these photos, and whose design makes this book a delight to read.

To Steve Legato, whose talent as a food photographer is only matched by his great taste in jazz.

To Anna Hampton, the gifted food stylist who made all of these libations and nibbles come alive for photography, and her assistant (as well as husband) Rob Hampton.

To Kristi Hunter, whose role of prop stylist included dozens and dozens of various glasses.

To Ed Claflin, my agent, for his constant support, encouragement, and humor.

To my dear family for their love and support, especially to Nancy and Walter Dubler; Ariela Dubler; Jesse Furman; Ilan, Mira, and Lev Dubler-Furman; Joshua Dubler; Lisa Cerami; Zahir and Charlie Cerami; David Krimm and Peter Bradley.

To many friends who enthusiastically volunteered to be taste testers and provided moral support, including Constance Brown, Kenn Speiser, Fox Wetle, Richard Besdine, Vicki Veh, Joe Chazan, Kim Montour, Nick Brown, Bruce Tillinghast, Sylvia Brown, Andrew West, and Bob Oates.

And to Patches and Rufous, my wonderful feline companions, who kept me company from their perches in the office and endorsed all the fish and seafood snacks when permitted.

Introduction

I'd much rather savor savories than swoon on sweets. Given the choice, I'd pack potato chips into my piehole long before pie. And that's why I love Bloody Marys.

There—in one frosty glass—almost all of my favorite food groups are represented. Salty? Yup, and that makes the brain release oxytocin, a hormone also triggered by sexual satisfaction. Spicy? In at least three ways if you count ground pepper and hot red pepper sauce as two and then add in horseradish for good measure. Something sour like lemon juice or pickle brine to make my lips pucker? You betcha! And then there's the base. It's tomato—at least most of the time—which is my favorite fruit juice.

If you pick your garnishes wisely you can include another important food: fat. A strip of crisp bacon laid across the top of a glass or a skewer of grilled sausage adds additional salt *plus* fat. And if you want to consider your garnishes healthy, the Bloody Mary and tuna fish salad are the two justifications for the existence of celery as a food.

There's culinary artistry that goes into creating a world-class Bloody. You don't just pour in two fingers of bourbon, add ice cubes, and top it with a splash of branch water. A great Bloody Mary has a distinctive flavor profile; there are layers upon layers of flavors that play off of each other and build to a crescendo of happiness. The drink is balanced like a masterful sauce.

Bloody Marys require a recipe. A description is hardly sufficient. Ratios don't do the trick because there are too many ingredients for four-to-one to have any meaning. In fact, I'll go so far as to assert that bad cooks can't invent a great Bloody Mary.

Bloody Marys can elicit snickers in some circles because they've so often been identified as a remedy for a hangover. Hangover libations are nothing new; back in the Middle Ages they drank a raw egg mixed into beer with lots of black pepper. We could say that the Bloody Mary is a new kid on the block because tomatoes were considered poisonous until the eighteenth century.

There are many nutrients in a traditional Bloody Mary. Salt and spices replace lost electrolytes, while the vitamin C, vitamin B6, and lycopene ease the havoc that overindulgence has wrought on the body.

Then, of course, there's a bit of alcohol. But there's no consensus within the medical community if that brings help or harm to the situation. Many scientists believe you're better off with the Virgin Mary.

My association with Bloody Marys is not as a curative, but rather as a festive beverage to share with convivial friends around a table. It's the best drink to pair with many of my favorite foods, most of which are served in the morning or at midday.

A plate of eggs Benedict topped with a rich hollandaise sauce, crêpes stuffed with shrimp curry, or a Western omelet dotted with bits of ham, onion, and bell pepper go with a Bloody Mary the way rack of lamb pairs with an aged Bordeaux. It can't be beaten. A mimosa or screwdriver just doesn't compare.

A basket of tender and flaky biscuits right out of the oven begs for something spicy to perk the palate, or if it's somewhat later in the day, you can't beat a Bloody Mary as the perfect drink with herbed focaccia or a plate of deviled eggs.

This book starts with the classics, because, as with music, you really have to master those before you can move on to improvisational jazz. There are recipes for a wide spectrum of traditional Bloody Mary mixes, and there's even a section on the best-tasting bottled versions. One of the trends today is flavored vodka, which is easy to make as a DIY project using real ingredients. You can infuse your booze with everything from citrus fruits to something as unexpected as smoky bacon, and you'll learn how on page 41.

What follows are two chapters of Bloody Mary recipes that may have certain ingredients recognizable from or related to a traditional Bloody Mary, but that take off in different directions. In Chapter 4 not all the drinks are even red—a few of them are crystal clear but still taste like a Bloody Mary. It's not alchemy; it's called careful straining. Interspersed with the drinks are easy-to-prepare recipes for bar snacks, because all sipping goes better with something to nosh.

The book concludes with a chapter on garnishes. Although the basic recipes have changed little in what is almost a century of sipping, the presentation of the drink has gone from minimalist to massive. Garnishes with the heft of Mount Rushmore of have replaced the traditional celery stick and lemon wedge: think gingery pickled carrots, maple bacon, and cubes of marinated ceviche.

Bloody Mary bars are quickly replacing ice cream sundae bars as a way to thrill guests at a get-together. Instead of bowls of sauces, crushed cookies, and chocolate sprinkles, partygoers can choose from five different types of pickles, flavored bacon, and cubes of salami and Swiss cheese. It's like letting adults loose in a candy store to watch the enjoyment around the table. And why not? Bloody Marys are meant to be enjoyed, especially with a group of friends.

So give your Bloody Marys a boost! Happy cooking!

Ellen Brown
Providence, Rhode Island

Fernand "Pete" Petiot, inventor of the Bloody Mary

CHAPTER 1

The Bloody Mary: A Drink of Legend and Lore

The parentage of Americans' favorite drinks is frequently shrouded with uncertainty and controversy, but there is more consensus about the Bloody Mary than there is about the mint julep or even the whiskey sour.

Most food and drink historians, although they take a circuitous route, come back to the now-legendary Fernand "Pete" Petiot, who was the bartender at Harry's New York Bar, which was located at 5 rue Danou in Paris. The watering hole, which is not related to the Harry's Bar in Venice that has the Bellini as its claim to fame, was opened in 1911 by Harry MacElhone. In a city filled with shining zinc bar tops made from galvanized steel, this was a New York–style bar with a wooden surface that had been dismantled and shipped across the Atlantic.

Around 1920 Russian émigrés began arriving in Paris after fleeing the revolution, and with them came both caviar and—more importantly—vodka. Petiot began playing around with the clear spirit, and declared it tasteless; they obviously brought the good stuff. At just the same time canned tomato juice reached Paris, and he started playing with the two, adding various other flavors and substances until his patrons declared it a hit. Thus, the Bloody Mary was born, and it appealed to some of his regular customers like Ernest Hemingway. It was first called the Bucket of Blood, named for a Chicago nightclub. And Americans fleeing Prohibition loved it and brought back tales of the drink to their alcohol-starved countrymen.

In the 1970s supporters of the antiwar movement were referred to as the doves, while those backing the war in Vietnam were called the hawks. Back in nineteenth-century America we had the wets versus the drys, and the issue was bourbon, not bullets.

Starting in the mid-nineteenth century a coalition was formed of rural Protestants and social Progressives regardless of their affiliation as Democrats or Republicans, and in the early twentieth century these groups were joined by the Woman's Christian Temperance Union to become the Anti-Saloon League. The emphasis was to ban alcohol state by state, and after most of the nation had gone dry, the Eighteenth Amendment, known as the Volstead Act, set down the rules for enforcing the ban on alcoholic beverages. The act was ratified in 1920, and for thirteen years was the law of the land—sort of. In truth, what the nation missed out on was not liquor but the tax revenues it generated when sold legally. In many ways it was seen as a conflict between rural Protestants and urban Catholics.

The act itself had the appearance of Swiss cheese. Wine used in a religious context was fine, and physicians could prescribe liquor for their patients.

The lack of legal sale gave rise to a whole new industry of illegal operators—the bootleggers. Urban crime rates soared as organized crime codified the bootleg liquor market, and the Volstead Act proved impossible to enforce. The speakeasy replaced the saloon. The Volstead Act went into effect on January 17, 1920, and within an hour, there were police reports of its having been broken.

In 1933 Congress proposed the Twenty-First Amendment to repeal Prohibition.

Although the national law was no longer in force, states and counties retained the right to set limits on or ban the sale of alcoholic beverages.

A Queen Dubbed Bloody Mary

With all of the attention paid to her father, King Henry VIII, and her younger sister, who reigned as Queen Elizabeth I, Queen Mary I has become almost a footnote in the history books. But she is the one whose nickname for the ages has been Bloody Mary.

Born in 1516, Mary was the only surviving child of Henry and his first wife, Catherine of Aragon. After her parents' marriage was annulled—because Henry had yet to start the Church of England that would provide him with future divorces—Mary was declared illegitimate.

Five wives later when Henry VIII died in 1547, the crown was passed to his only son. King Edward VI was just ten years old at the time, and died a mere six years later but not before he had set a plan in place to exclude his two half-sisters from the line of succession. His choice instead was Lady Jane Grey, a distant relative who was the granddaughter of Henry's younger sister, who ruled for nine days before she was overthrown by Mary in 1553.

Mary remained a devout Roman Catholic and gained her sanguine nickname for the executions she ordered of Protestant clergy while trying to link England once again to the papacy. Her targets included Thomas Cranmer, archbishop of Canterbury, among countless others. Mary was thirty-seven at the time of her accession, and she was desperate to produce a Catholic heir so the throne would not go to her Protestant sister, Elizabeth, upon her death.

She married King Philip II of Spain and remained childless. There were reports of two "false pregnancies" during which she gained weight but no child was born, and historians now believe these were ectopic pregnancies. Mary died five years into her reign in 1558.

"Bloody Mary" was also memorialized in the children's nursery rhyme: "Mary, Mary, quite contrary, how does your garden grow? With silver bells and cockle shells and pretty maids all in a row." History disagrees on the actual significance of the bells, shells, and maids: The bells could represent church bells; the shells may be a nod to Saint James, whose symbol is the scallop shell; and the maids could be Catholic nuns. But other interpretations tie the silver bells to Mary's elaborate dresses, the shells to her fondness for exotic foods, and the maids to her ladies-in-waiting.

After the implementation of the Twenty-First Amendment the bar scene in the United States could once again thrive, and in 1933 Petiot moved to New York City after being wooed by industrialist Vincent Astor to head the King Cole Bar at the landmark Hotel St. Regis, known for its dominating mural by American illustrator Maxfield Parrish. But there his drink was called the Red Snapper, and a "secret ingredient" was a dash of vodka in which a handful of black peppercorns had marinated for more than a month. The media made the drink a darling, and it gained the status of a classic.

In most of the country the drink had become the Bloody Mary, with a reference to Queen Mary I of England and Ireland, who was known for her reign of terror against the countries' Protestants. Smirnoff started distilling vodka in 1934, when the ink on the Twenty-First Amendment was barely dry, when Russian immigrant Rudolph Kunnetchansky founded the company. There was an instant marriage between his product and the Bloody Mary, although vaudevillian George "Georgie" Jessel claims that the Mary in question was not a queen but his friend Mary Geraghty. Other stories say it was named after film diva Mary Pickford.

In an interview with the *New Yorker* in 1964, Petiot said that Jessel's claim was a simple brew of half vodka and half tomato juice, and it was he who added the salt, pepper, lemon, and Worcestershire sauce. No one has come forward to claim either the horseradish or the celery salt.

In 1942 *Life* magazine printed a recipe similar to a Bloody Mary but it was called the Red Hammer. The earliest recipe we can find for a Bloody Mary under its real name was printed in 1946, and many bars around the country claim to have added the celery stick as an edible swizzle stick.

Following World War II, when suburban living became the new Holy Grail, the Bloody Mary was already firmly ensconced as the leading drink to serve for brunch, a meal period that was new to the country. Although thought of by some as a hangover cure, the drink is most often associated with the convivial spirit of a brunch party.

THERE'S A CATCHY TUNE BY THAT NAME, TOO

The name was so popular that Rodgers and Hammerstein chose it for a character in their musical that opened in 1949, *South Pacific*. Bloody Mary is a Tonkinese woman who makes a living selling trinkets to the sailors, and is the subject of a rousing musical number in the first act, when the sailors belt out the lyrics "Bloody Mary is the girl I love, her skin is tender as DiMaggio's glove." The musical is based on *Tales of the South Pacific*, the first major novel written by James A. Michener that was published in 1947 and won the Pulitzer Prize a year later.

The biggest boost to the popularity of Bloody Marys could be traced to the introduction of a great convenience food—bottled Bloody Mary mixers. It was Herb and June Taylor who became Mr. and Mrs. T and introduced their product through food-service channels in 1960. The brand's real break came a few years later when it was adopted in the small cans familiar to all airline passengers. It was the customers who then demanded that grocery stores carry it.

And that brings us to today. Bloody Marys are the go-to drink for the early part of the day, but their variations—especially the exciting hand-crafted drinks like the recipes in this book—are becoming increasingly popular at all times of day.

Telling the Future via Bloody Mary

Bloody Mary is also a lesser character rooted in nineteenth-century American folklore that ranges from benign to truly malevolent depending on which version of the tale is being told. Whether she's a ghost, phantom, or spirit, she is credited with the ability to reveal the future if conjured.

The ritual, primarily performed by young girls in order to see a vision of their future husband, is about as eerie and creepy as a haunted house. In one version the girls walk backward up the stairs in a darkened house with a mirror in one hand and a candle in the other. An alternative scenario is that a group of young women ritualistically call out her name in a dimly lit room.

If all goes well, they're supposed to catch a glimpse of their future husband. But it's not that easy. Sometimes they would see a skull or the face of the Grim Reaper; this is a sign that they're going to die before marriage.

But that's not the only thing to fear. Instead of being a harmless apparition, Bloody Mary can be evil; she is said to scream, or have the power to strangle or drink the blood of those who seek her. Not nearly as nice as a cocktail.

CHAPTER 2

Anatomy of the Ideal Bloody Mary

To bring luck to a bride, her white gown is supposed to be accented by items drawn from the rather broad categories of "something old, something new, something borrowed, and something blue." To bring happiness to the lips of a person sipping a traditional Bloody Mary, a parallel phrase for augmenting the tomato juice would be "something spicy, something salty, something tangy, and something complex." And then, of course, there's adding a jigger or two of liquor.

In both cases, there's a lot of latitude within these categories. And in this chapter you're going learn about all of the various foods that glorify the flavor of tomato juice, starting with an exploration of the juice itself.

Regal Options for the
Red Juice Component

You'll find recipes in Chapter 4 that aren't red at all. Some are green, others are yellow, and then a few are perfectly clear. But to most people a Bloody Mary is a red drink based on tomato juice or mixed vegetable juice such as V8, which is dominated by tomato juice.

After you make your own cooked tomato juice you'll be spoiled forever, but it's always good to have a bottle in the pantry. To determine the best brand, a group of friends and I got together one afternoon and tried eight juices commonly found across the country—you might say we got a lycopene overload.

The overall winner was R. W. Knudsen Family Organic Tomato Juice; it has the deep flavor of tomatoes ripened on the vine with a texture that is rich enough not to become wimpy when diluted with liquor and ice, but not so thick that you want to chew it when drinking it plain.

Our second-place winner, and not far below the organic juice, was Campbell's Tomato Juice, which is about half the price of the R. W. Knudsen drink. It really tastes like ripe tomatoes.

While these two were on the top of the tomato totem pole, other juices we found acceptable were produced by Welch's, Del Monte, Sacramento, and the 365 Everyday Value brand sold at Whole Foods Market.

But none of the commercial juices held a candle to this homemade juice.

Cooked Tomato Juice

The celery and herbs simmered with the tomatoes just glorify the juice's sweet flavor; you really don't distinguish them individually.

Makes about 1 quart

3 pounds very ripe red tomatoes, cored and diced
¾ cup diced celery, including the leaves
1 shallot, minced
3 tablespoons chopped fresh basil leaves
2 sprigs fresh thyme
1 bay leaf
2 teaspoons kosher salt
Freshly ground black pepper
Hot red pepper sauce

Combine the tomatoes, celery, shallot, basil, thyme, bay leaf, salt, black pepper to taste, and ¾ cup water in a nonreactive saucepan. Bring to a boil over medium heat, then lower the heat and simmer the mixture, uncovered and stirring occasionally, for 30 minutes.

Remove and discard the bay leaf. Force the mixture through a strainer, pressing with the back of a spoon to extract as much liquid as possible; alternatively use a food mill fitted with the grinding disk that has the smallest holes.

Season to taste with hot red pepper sauce. Transfer the juice to a storage container and refrigerate, tightly covered. Once chilled, adjust the seasoning if necessary.

Notes: The juice can be refrigerated for up to 5 days.

Even when straining a liquid, it's worth it to take the time to discard the bay leaf. Bits of the bitter herb can make it through even the small holes of a food mill.

The Italian Secret Weapon: Passata di Pomodoro

Texture is the key to a truly exceptional Bloody Mary, and what most serious mixologists hold as the gold standard is a drink that retains the smooth, slightly thick, and velvety mouthfeel of tomato juice. That's not as easy as it sounds when you consider that the viscous red liquid is thinned out by myriad ingredients—from the liquor itself and the melting ice to citrus juice, Worcestershire sauce, and hot red pepper sauce.

A secret ingredient to achieve that rich texture is a stalwart of the Italian home kitchen rarely used on this side of the Atlantic. Called *passata di pomodoro* in Italian, it's basically just ground-up tomatoes that have been strained to rid it of the pesky seeds and skin, so it delivers a real tomato hit.

Many of the Italian imports are sold in tall glass bottles that resemble wine carafes; aseptic boxes of passata, both imported and made domestically, are also now available.

Passata may look a lot like tomato sauce, but appearance is where the similarity stops. Tomato sauce achieves its texture by reduction and its flavor from additional ingredients that can range from herbs and spices to carrots and onions. If anything passata is closer to tomato paste, which is just tomatoes that are cooked for hours to drastically reduce the amount of liquid. But tomato paste never regains a sense of fresh flavor.

Although passata di pomodoro is called strained tomatoes, the tomatoes do go through a minimal amount of cooking to break them down enough to strain, in the same way they are exposed to heat to peel them.

If you can't find bottled passata, or don't want to make it yourself, the best substitute is to drain whole canned tomatoes, reserving the juice. Purée the tomatoes and add some of the juice to achieve a thick yet pourable consistency.

Strained Tomatoes
(Passata di Pomodoro)

Here's the easy method for making this "utility infielder" yourself. In addition to using it in Bloody Marys, you can sub it into any recipe requiring crushed tomatoes or sauce.

Makes about 1 quart

3 pounds ripe plum tomatoes, cored and halved
 lengthwise
1 teaspoon kosher salt
2 fresh basil leaves (optional)

Place the tomatoes and salt in a saucepan. Cover the pan and bring to a simmer over medium heat, stirring occasionally. Simmer the tomatoes for 5 minutes, or until they start to soften.

Pour the tomatoes into a food mill fitted with the grinding disk that has the smallest holes or into a strainer set over a mixing bowl. Allow the tomatoes to sit for 5 minutes. Drain any liquid that has accumulated in the mixing bowl, and save it for another use such as in a soup or stew.

Rotate the handle of the food mill to purée the tomatoes until only the skins and seeds remain; alternatively, force the tomatoes through the strainer with the back of a spoon, pressing to extract as much liquid as possible.

Transfer the purée to a storage container, adding a few basil leaves, if desired.

Note: The passata can be refrigerated for up to 5 days or frozen for up to 6 months.

Something Spicy:
Hot Sauces

Years back a definition of longevity was being so old that you had to buy a second bottle of Tabasco sauce. But Americans today like their food spicy, not only including but especially their Bloody Marys.

Tabasco, which has been around since 1868 and is still produced on Louisiana's Avery Island, controlled the market for decades. In fact, Tabasco is to the hot red pepper sauce category as Kleenex is to facial tissues and Formica is to plastic laminates; it's a trademarked brand that is used widely as a generic. Although companies like Frank's RedHot claim to be the sauce used in the authentic Buffalo chicken wings, Frank's is still a basic recipe of mashed red chile peppers with vinegar and salt.

It appears that most cuisines in tropical areas where chile peppers are grown have a sauce tailored to that country's favorite dishes; these condiments are more complexly flavored than American "hot red pepper sauce." More and more we are turning to an international array of products that all deliver a peppery punch. Here's an overview of some popular options.

Sriracha sauce: Although sriracha has been manufactured since 1980, it wasn't until this decade that it became mainstreamed into American life. Pronounced *see-ROTCH-ahh* as if the first *r* wasn't there, sriracha is now flavoring everything from potato chips to Heinz Ketchup, and in most supermarkets it's shelved with the hot sauces rather than the Asian ingredients. The mélange of chile peppers, sugar, salt, garlic powder, and distilled white vinegar (using xanthan gum as a thickening agent and potassium sorbate and sodium bisulfite as preservatives) really has no parentage in a specific Asian cuisine.

How to Handle
Temperamental Tomatoes

The chef's knives fly when the topic arises about what is the best way to handle fresh tomatoes, on which many of the Bloody Mary mix recipes in this book depend.

Although storage is a thorny issue, there seems to be consensus that tomatoes should be ripened with their stem end down. When tomatoes are pulled from the vine, it injures the fruit and causes a scar. If the stem end is placed down, the "shoulders" of the tomato protect it and keep bacteria at bay. The exception to the rule: If the tomato has some of the stem attached, it should be ripened with the stem end up as its crown.

Now we come to storage. In an ideal world everyone has a wine cellar or wine refrigerator that is kept at 53°F to 55°F, and once the tomatoes have ripened they are transferred to that ideal temperature. But realism now rears its ugly head.

If tomatoes are stored at colder than 50°F, according to a study done by the French National Institute for Agricultural Research, the sugar content and acidity remain the same, but the tomatoes lose their grassy aroma and the flesh can become mealy. But tomatoes rot if kept at summer room temperature, 85°F, which it can often be the case in our kitchens.

My answer is to buy just a few ripe or almost ripe tomatoes at a time and keep them at room temperature. But it's better to eat less aromatic tomatoes than to throw out rotten ones.

The Spotlight on Sriracha

Huy Fong Foods began making Sriracha Hot Chili Sauce in 1980, when David Tran, a Vietnamese transplant of Chinese ancestry, started producing it in Rosemead, a town in California's San Gabriel Valley. Tran was born in 1945, the Year of the Rooster in the Chinese zodiac, and he started manufacturing chile sauce in Vietnam prior to his immigration. Even ten years ago it was referred to as "red rooster sauce" because of the image of a majestic white fowl emblazoned on the clear plastic bottle, penned in by text in Vietnamese, Chinese, English, French, and Spanish.

Red jalapeño chiles are the source of the heat and color, but the flavor is complex and rounded. That's why so many chefs adopted it in place of Tabasco or other hot red pepper sauces. In 2010 *Bon Appétit* magazine named it ingredient of the year. And its popularity continues to skyrocket.

Gochujang: This Korean sauce, pronounced *kah-chu-yang*, dates back to the eighteenth century and it is an integral part of Korean life and cuisine. The primary ingredients are red chile powder, glutinous rice powder mixed with fermented soybeans, and salt. There's always a bit of sweetener added to the dark-reddish paste, which gives it a rich flavor. Gochujang adds richness as well as heat to a Bloody Mary. Make it the first addition to your tomato juice and stir it well before adding other flavorings.

Sambal oelek: Native to the Malay Peninsula and Indonesia, this sauce, pronounced *SAM-bell OH-lek*, traditionally blends the red chile peppers with varied ingredients like shrimp paste, fish sauce, garlic, ginger, shallot, scallion, and tomato tempered by a range of acids including lime juice and vinegars balanced by sugar. The most common chiles used are habañero, cayenne, and bird's eye. That's a lot of flavor in one small bottle, and all are great nuances in a Bloody Mary.

Harissa: Harissa is the national condiment in Tunisia, but it is used over the whole region of North Africa. In addition to chile peppers, the base contains roasted red bell pepper that is combined with aromatic spices like coriander and cumin and flavored with onion and garlic as well as a bit of tomato. Because the ingredients are very common, this is one sauce that's easy to make at home, so I've given you a recipe. Harissa, pronounced *har-EE-sah*, is used as an ingredient far more than as a condiment.

Peri-peri sauce: This sauce is most closely associated with Portugal's former holdings in southern Africa, including Mozambique, Angola, and the Cape Verde Islands where peri-peri (or piri-piri) chiles are grown. The sauce blends the crushed peppers with citrus zest, onion, pepper, salt, lemon juice, bay leaves, and paprika; some brands also include additional European herbs like basil, oregano, and tarragon. These additional ingredients add complex flavor to a Bloody Mary.

Pickapeppa Sauce: It's finally time to scan the shelves for hot products from the New World, because the chile pepper's lineage starts here. Pickapeppa Sauce was developed in Jamaica in 1921, and it has a flavor profile that is sweet-and-sour and only mildly spicy, especially when compared with the sauces from other parts of the world. It's made from peppers blended with vinegar, sugar, tomatoes, raisins, ginger, and onion, which are then flavored with orange zest, cloves, and thyme. Because it won't make you breathe fire, it can be used as a general condiment, and I highly recommend it in the Muddled Masterpiece (page 85).

Cholula Hot Sauce: If Tabasco sauce is known for its stylized perfume-type bottles, this south-of-the-border contender boasts a round wooden top as its emblem. Now owned by tequila giant Jose Cuervo, the sauce is native to the Jalisco region of Mexico where it was a key ingredient in sangrita, a blend of citrus juices used as a chaser for shots of tequila. Pronounced *cho-LOU-lah*, it wasn't introduced into the United States until 1989, and soon became the darling of Mexican-food aficionados. The ingredients are a combination of pequín chile and chile de árbol blended with spices and vinegar.

The only ingredient uniting these sauces is at least one type of chile pepper, but all types contain capsaicin, which is what causes the burning sensation in the mouth. What happens is that the body defends against the pain sensation by secreting endorphins, which are natural painkillers. It's not the supposed runner's high, but chile heads don't care.

THE SCOVILLE SCALE QUANTIFIES THE HEAT

Writers like Robert Parker quantify the quality of wines by assigning them a numerical value, with anything more than a 90 considered coveted by any and all vintners. It was an American pharmacist, Wilbur Scoville, who did something similar for chile peppers in 1912, and the Scoville Scale is still used to measure their heat levels today. The higher the number of Scoville heat units (SHU), the hotter the pepper. Like Parker's ratings, the test of hotness is imprecise because of variations in the subjects' palates as well as sensory fatigue—the palate desensitizes rapidly after a few assaults.

Harissa

Although the sauce is now easy to find in stores, there's a richness and aromatic quality to homemade harissa that makes it worth the time to prepare your own. If you can't find red jalapeño chiles use green ones and let them sit around for a few days to turn red.

Makes about ¾ cup

1 large red bell pepper
1 teaspoon ground coriander
1 teaspoon ground cumin
2 tablespoons olive oil
½ small red onion, chopped
3 garlic cloves, minced
3 red jalapeño chiles, seeds and ribs removed, chopped
2 tablespoons freshly squeezed lemon juice
1 tablespoon tomato paste
Salt

Prepare a charcoal or gas grill or preheat the broiler. Broil the bell pepper, turning it with tongs, for 15 minutes, or until the skin is uniformly charred and the flesh softens. Transfer the pepper to a heavy, resealable plastic bag and allow it to cool. Peel the pepper under cold running water, and discard the peel and seeds.

While the pepper cools, place a dry skillet over low heat and toast the coriander and cumin for 1 minute, or until fragrant. Scrape the spices from the skillet into a food processor.

Heat the oil in the skillet over medium heat. Add the onion, garlic, and chiles and cook, stirring frequently, for 8 to 10 minutes, or until browned.

Place the bell pepper and vegetables in the food processor, and add the lemon juice and tomato paste. Process until a smooth paste forms, season with salt to taste, and scrape the mixture into a storage container.

Note: The harissa can be refrigerated for up to 2 weeks in an airtight container.

The Other Kind of Spicy: Horseradish and Wasabi

Though the range of products that come from chile peppers, not to mention the peppers themselves, all deliver heat, there's a complementary family of plants that deliver a more pungent—though not any milder—burn. The best-known of these is horseradish. While chiles are all part of the *Capsicum* genus, horseradish belongs to the Brassicaceae family, which includes equally pungent mustard and wasabi as well as mild members like cabbage and broccoli.

It's the fiery flecks of horseradish grated from this root that transform tomato-based chili sauce into cocktail sauce. And we look for them as well when a Bloody Mary is set before us.

The root itself, like an uncut chile pepper, has almost no aroma. But unlike with chile peppers, which you must experience up close to feel the spice level, just being in the vicinity of a horseradish root being grated will make you aware of its kick. When its cell walls are broken down, allyl isothiocyanate—a form of mustard gas—is produced, which may cause irritation of the eyes and mucous membranes in the nose and sinuses.

For horseradish, there's no equivalent to the Scoville Scale that measures the heat of chile peppers. It's pretty much all the same. Horseradish is mentioned in literature from antiquity, and by the Middle Ages it was used as a medicine. But by the sixteenth century it had wended its way from the medicine chest to the dinner table and had been adopted as a condiment all across Europe. Both Thomas Jefferson and George Washington planted horseradish in their gardens for culinary uses.

It's rare for a recipe for a Bloody Mary or any other dish to specify freshly grated horseradish; almost all recipes use its handy prepared variety that is already mixed with a bit of vinegar and salt. Should you see a reference to freshly grated horseradish, substitute one-and-a-half-times the amount of prepared horseradish to achieve the same level of pungency. And if you're grating fresh horseradish always make sure the wind is at your back.

Some prepared horseradish has beets included to create a shocking pink color. This is used most often as an accompaniment to gefilte fish at Jewish holiday dinners or smeared on a sandwich, but is rarely included in cooking or in mixing a Bloody Mary.

The What and Where of Wasabi

No visit to a sushi bar would be complete without a dollop of fluorescent green wasabi swimming in a saucer of soy sauce. Also called Japanese horseradish, wasabi is a first cousin to horseradish and is a bit sharper in flavor.

I hate to break the magic spell, but unless you're holding out for the Easter bunny and the tooth fairy, the chances that you've eaten authentic wasabi are fairly small. That is unless you trekked the streambeds in particularly mountainous parts of Japan to collect this rare rhizome.

Real wasabi contains the same allyl isothiocyanate as horseradish, and in greater concentration. Though horseradish is generally grated rather coarsely, wasabi is grated as finely as possible, traditionally by a piece of shark's skin. But its potency lasts for only a few minutes.

What we know as wasabi is a mixture of horseradish, mustard, and green food coloring. That is, unless you shop online. Real Wasabi is a firm in Bluffton, South Carolina, that grows and ships authentic wasabi (www.realwasabi.com), plus you can find a few other brands' products listed on Amazon.com.

A Bit of Bitters?

Bitters are like having a spice rack at your bar. These bitter and sour blends, which you use very sparingly, are flavored with aromatic herbs, bark, roots, and some fruits. They've been around since the ancient Egyptians, and the British started using them as preventive medicine back in the eighteenth century.

There are two kinds of bitters. Digestive bitters like Italian Campari and Fernet-Branca or German Underberg are served straight up or on the rocks at the end of a meal to aid in digestion.

What we put in a Bloody Mary is termed cocktail bitters. The reason why they can be sold in supermarkets is that they are classified in this country as "alcoholic non-beverage products" meaning that the dash or splash you put in a drink doesn't count.

Bitters were an integral ingredient in cocktails until the evil era of Prohibition wiped them out, and after its repeal only a few old stalwarts like Angostura and Peychaud's bounced back, for making Manhattans and rounding out Sazeracs. But the rise of our new cocktail culture, including the renaissance of the Bloody Mary, has led to many new flavors on the market and a bunch of new boutique companies making them: The Bitter Truth, Fee Brothers, and Bittermens, among others, produce wonderful products.

The one specified most often in this book is celery bitters; it's the yin to celery salt's yang. The other one used is orange bitters, which adds the same sort of essence as a sprinkling of zest.

That Salty Sensation

Even though most commercial tomato juice and bottled Bloody Mary mixes contain a lot of sodium, almost all of us add something salty to the drink. Sometimes a few ingredients—like a combination of celery salt and Worcestershire sauce—are paired to deliver a salt stomp in different ways.

Most sauces also add complexity to the flavor of the drink because they contain other flavorful components in addition to sodium, but there are some that just pack in the salt, so use them more sparingly. Here's a summary of various options that all work well in Bloody Marys.

Worcestershire sauce: This British invention is clearly the most popular of the group and is included in almost every recipe for Bloody Mary mix. The reason why it's *almost* every recipe is because it contains anchovies, which makes it incompatible with vegan and some vegetarian diets. In addition to a few kinds of vinegar and anchovies, the sauce contains tamarind extract, onions, garlic, sugar, and peppers.

A.1. Original Sauce: Even older than Worcestershire sauce is this condiment for meats, developed by Henderson William Brand, a chef to King George IV of England, in 1824. It was first bottled in 1831 and its ingredients overlap with many of those in Worcestershire sauce, but it also includes tomatoes, raisin paste, and puréed orange. The thick texture of this steak sauce makes it an excellent addition to Bloody Marys because it resists dilution.

Anchovy paste: Anchovies are about as polarizing as cilantro (see page 131) but when it comes to the salty paste, a little goes a long way in delivering not only salinity but also that intangible savory umami quality. Most of the time when I use it in Bloody Marys and other cooking it's not discernable as anchovy to even anchovy haters, nor is it visible.

Thai or Vietnamese fish sauce (nam pla): Like anchovy paste, this clear amber-colored liquid cannot be added to a drink if it's for a vegan or some vegetarians, but it adds salt plus a zingy finish that is part fish and part just savory umami.

Soy sauce: Soy sauce dates back to the second century CE, and we're all familiar with it as a condiment common in all Asian cuisines. It's also a great addition to Bloody Marys, especially if some of the other flavoring ingredients are pulled from that same pantry. Traditional soy sauce is a fermented product made by mixing soybeans and grain with mold cultures such as *Aspergillus oryzae* and yeasts. The mixture was then allowed to ferment in the sun for many months. People following a gluten-free diet should be aware that many brands of soy sauce are not acceptable, but many leading brands, such as Kikkoman, now make gluten-free soy.

Bragg Liquid Aminos: If you desire a salty sensation in your Bloody Mary but really want to cut back on the amount of sodium in your diet, trek to an Asian market or health food store for Bragg Liquid Aminos. It's a liquid protein concentrate that comes from soybeans, but it's all-natural, contains no gluten, and has far less sodium than other options. And it's been around for more than a century, so it's not a new kid on the block.

There Really Was a Mr. Lea and a Mr. Perrins

Fermented fish sauces date back to the Greco-Roman times, and we have evidence from reports in the Middle Ages that they never went away. But the introduction of Lea & Perrins Sauce in 1837 has a muddy history. Some claim that its parentage goes back to a sauce encountered by a noble from Worcestershire while he was governor of Bengal, but others maintain it was a domestic invention. It was two pharmacists (dubbed chemists in England), John Wheeley Lea and William Henry Perrins, who mixed up a batch. Apparently it was terrible and the barrel languished in the basement for a few years. When they tried it again it had fermented into a delicious brew, and so the first bottling happened.

The Taste of Tangy

The last category of products on the flavor spectrum of a typical Bloody Mary is something tangy loaded with acid. Most of the time it's the freshly squeezed juice from lemons and limes, and occasionally even grapefruit.

But there are other options. Many of these recipes call for a food that's basically free: the brine in which olives and pickles are packed that everyone pours down the drain. What I like so much about especially pickle brine is that is includes other flavors as well; there can be anything from sprigs of aromatic fresh dill to cloves of garlic.

The final group of acids that are very well suited to Bloody Marys is a range of vinegars from the soft end of the spectrum or harsher potions used in small quantities. I'm especially fond of unseasoned rice vinegar if the drink draws from Asian flavors, and balsamic vinegar adds a sweet note along with its acidic punch. If using red or white wine vinegar, add it slowly because the level of acidity differs from brand to brand.

Infused Liquor for Handcrafted Appeal

Infusing alcohol goes back centuries, but it's also part of today's hip-and-happening DIY scene. In fact, flavored liquor, along with homemade bitters, is a cornerstone in the craft cocktail movement that began around the turn of the century when a whole new generation "discovered" such classic drinks as martinis and Bloody Marys.

Now every bar touts its drink list with a degree of snobbery formerly reserved for a wine list filled with first-growth Bordeaux.

There's very little skill needed to infuse booze, and the results are delicious. You can pour them over some ice cubes or use them in more complex mixed drinks; you'll find they add a subtle nuance to the flavor of the Bloody Mary. And because of the high alcohol percentage of the base liquor there are no fears of bacteria forming, as is a concern when infusing oils. You should drink the infused liquor within six months, but know that the flavor will lessen over time.

The most common liquor for flavoring is by far vodka, but you can also use gin, rum, pisco, and tequila. The variables are how much flavoring you add and how long you leave it in the bottle to infuse its flavor. What I frequently do is draw out a sample after a few days and taste it to determine if additional steeping time is needed.

As a general rule I use two cups of chopped fruit to a 750-mililiter bottle of liquor. Herbs and spices also make excellent flavors: Herbs should be bruised to release their essential oils, and spices like cinnamon sticks and star anise should be toasted before they're soaked.

Bacon-Infused Vodka

Makes 1 (750 ml) bottle

8 ounces thick-sliced bacon, cut into ¾-inch pieces
1 (750 ml) bottle vodka

Move a rack to the bottom third of the oven, and preheat the oven to 400°F. Line a rimmed baking sheet with heavy-duty aluminum foil, and arrange the bacon strips on the foil. Bake the bacon for 12 to 15 minutes, or until brown but still pliable; do not allow it to become crispy and do not allow the grease to burn.

Transfer the bacon and accumulated bacon grease to a 2-quart glass jar. Add the vodka, screw the lid on the jar tightly, and shake well. Allow the bacon to steep for 3 to 4 days at room temperature, shaking the jar a few times a day. Strain out the solids, pressing with the back of a spoon to extract as much liquid as possible.

Return the vodka to the jar and place it in the freezer for 4 hours to freeze the residual bacon grease. Line a sieve with a paper coffee filter or paper towel. Strain the vodka through the paper into a clean container. Return the vodka to the freezer for 4 hours and repeat the straining process. Use a funnel to pour the liquid back into the original bottle, and label it clearly.

Variation: Substitute tequila for the vodka and add 1 or 2 halved jalapeño or serrano chiles to the jar for 1 to 2 days. Then remove the chiles and allow the bacon to continue steeping.

Citrus Vodka

· ·

Makes 1 (750 ml) bottle

1 (750 ml) bottle vodka
1 small red grapefruit
1 lime
1 lemon

Place the vodka in a 2-quart glass jar. Wash the grapefruit, lime, and lemon with mild soap under warm running water. Cut the fruit into wedges and add them to the jar with the liquor. Screw the lid on the jar tightly, and allow the fruit to macerate for 2 to 4 days at room temperature. Strain out the solids, shaking them well in a sieve. Use a funnel to pour the liquid back into the original bottle, and label it clearly.

Variation: Substitute gin for the vodka.

Spicy Vodka

Makes 1 (750 ml) bottle

1 (750 ml) bottle vodka
2 to 4 jalapeño or serrano chiles, halved
6 garlic cloves, halved
1 tablespoon black peppercorns, coarsely crushed

Place the vodka in a 1-quart glass jar. For very spicy vodka, use the halved chiles with the seeds. For less spicy vodka, discard the seeds and ribs.

Add the chiles, garlic, and peppercorns to the vodka. Screw the lid on the jar tightly, and allow it to steep for 1 to 3 days at room temperature. Strain out the solids, pressing with the back of a spoon to extract as much liquid as possible. Use a funnel to pour the liquid back into the original bottle, and label it clearly.

Variation: Substitute tequila for the vodka.

Herbed Gin

· ·

Makes 1 (750 ml) bottle

1 (750 ml) bottle gin
4 sprigs fresh thyme
2 sprigs fresh rosemary
½ cup firmly packed fresh basil leaves

Place the gin in a 1-quart glass jar. Bruise the thyme, rosemary, and basil leaves by hitting them with the dull side of a knife or mashing them with a mortar and pestle or cocktail muddler.

Add the herbs to the gin, screw the lid on the jar tightly, and allow it to steep for 2 to 4 days at room temperature. Strain out the solids, pressing with the back of a spoon to extract as much liquid as possible. Use a funnel to pour the liquid back into the original bottle, and label it clearly.

Variation: Substitute vodka for the gin.

Note: The taste of herbs comes from the oils contained in the cell walls. Heating releases them, but for infusing flavor in an uncooked dish like this or salad dressings the herbs should be bruised.

Basic Bloody Mary Mixes

In the next two chapters of this book you'll find many unique and (I hope you think) delicious combinations for specific drinks. But most of the time you may just want to make the very best traditional Bloody Mary possible, one that will elicit oohs and aahs from friends from the very first sip. It must have all the recognizable families of ingredients—from tomatoey to spicy to tangy to salty. And all of these recipes can be personalized in myriad ways. While some ingredients like the tomato juice itself can come from a can or a bottle, freshly squeezed citrus juices are a must for all drinks, as is freshly ground black pepper.

Basic Bloody Mary Mix
with Canned Juice

This is the one that you can whip up quickly, although it's best if the flavors are allowed to blend. With the exception of squeezing some citrus fruits everything else is right in the pantry or refrigerator.

Makes about 1 quart

2½ cups tomato juice
½ cup strained tomatoes (passata di pomodoro) or an additional ½ cup tomato juice
¼ cup prepared white horseradish
2 tablespoons freshly squeezed lemon juice
2 tablespoons freshly squeezed lime juice
2 tablespoons Worcestershire sauce
2 tablespoons olive or pickle brine
1 teaspoon celery salt
1 teaspoon coarsely ground black pepper
1 teaspoon hot red pepper sauce, or more to taste

Combine the tomato juice, strained tomatoes, horseradish, lemon juice, lime juice, Worcestershire sauce, brine, celery salt, black pepper, and hot red pepper sauce in a 1-quart container. Shake well, and refrigerate for at least 4 hours, but preferably overnight.

Note: The mix can be made up to 2 days in advance and refrigerated, tightly covered.

Raw Tomato Bloody Mary Mix

. . . .

When I have a bumper crop of tomatoes in August this version is on the top of my list.

Makes about 1 quart

2½ pounds ripe red tomatoes, cored and diced
2 celery ribs with leaves, if possible, diced
½ cup firmly packed fresh parsley
1 tablespoon prepared white horseradish
2 tablespoons freshly squeezed lemon juice
2 teaspoons Worcestershire sauce
1½ teaspoons kosher salt
½ teaspoon celery seeds
½ teaspoon freshly ground black pepper, or more to taste
1 to 1½ teaspoons hot red pepper sauce, or more to taste

Combine the tomatoes, celery, parsley, horseradish, lemon juice, Worcestershire sauce, salt, celery seed, black pepper, and hot red pepper sauce in a food processor or blender. Purée until smooth.

Transfer the mixture to a mixing bowl and chill for at least 4 hours, but preferably overnight. Force the mixture through a strainer, pressing with the back of a spoon to extract as much liquid as possible; alternatively, use a food mill fitted with the grinding disk that has the smallest holes. Transfer the mix to a storage container and refrigerate.

Note: The mix can be made up to 2 days in advance and refrigerated, tightly covered.

Grilled Tomato Bloody Mary Mix

Roasted tomatoes and the addition of chipotle peppers and smoked salt add a smoky nuance to this mix.

Makes about 1 quart

4 pounds red tomatoes, halved and cored

2 lemons, halved

6 celery ribs

2 jalapeño or serrano chiles, halved, seeds and ribs removed

3 tablespoons Worcestershire sauce

1 tablespoon freshly grated horseradish (substitute 2 tablespoons prepared white horseradish)

1 chipotle in adobo sauce, diced

1 tablespoon superfine granulated sugar

2 teaspoons smoked salt

½ teaspoon coarsely ground black pepper

Prepare a charcoal or gas grill or preheat a cast-iron griddle pan. Place the tomatoes, lemons, celery, and chiles cut-side down on the grate. Grill for 4 to 5 minutes, or until the tomatoes are charred. Turn the celery ribs after 2 minutes.

Remove the ingredients from the grill. Place the tomatoes, celery, and chiles in a food processor or blender. Squeeze ¼ cup of juice from the lemons, and add it to the food processor along with the Worcestershire sauce, horseradish, chipotle, sugar, salt, and black pepper. Purée until smooth.

Force the mixture through a strainer, pressing with the back of a spoon to extract as much liquid as possible; alternatively, use a food mill fitted with the grinding disk that has the smallest holes. Refrigerate the mix for at least 4 hours, but preferably overnight.

Note: The mix can be made up to 2 days in advance and refrigerated, tightly covered.

Basic Bloody Caesar Mix

While there are a variety of bottled Bloody Mary mixes that are worthy of keeping around, there hasn't been the same attention paid to the stalwart of Canadian brunch drinks, the Bloody Caesar. Almost all bars in its country of origin as well as in the United States use bottled Clamato juice: seasoned tomato juice premixed with clam juice. Here's an easy-to-make alternative.

Makes about 1 quart

2 garlic cloves
1 large shallot, diced
1½ cups bottled clam juice, divided
1 cup strained tomatoes (passata di pomodoro)
½ cup tomato juice
¼ cup prepared white horseradish
2 tablespoons freshly squeezed lemon juice
2 tablespoons freshly squeezed lime juice
2 tablespoons Worcestershire sauce
2 tablespoons olive or pickle brine
1 teaspoon celery salt
1 teaspoon coarsely ground black pepper
1 teaspoon hot red pepper sauce, or more to taste

Combine the garlic, shallot, and ½ cup of the clam juice in a food processor or blender. Purée until smooth.

Transfer the mixture to a 1-quart container and add the remaining clam juice, strained tomatoes, tomato juice, horseradish, lemon juice, lime juice, Worcestershire sauce, brine, celery salt, black pepper, and hot red pepper sauce. Shake well, and refrigerate for at least 4 hours, but preferably overnight.

Note: The mix can be made up to 2 days in advance and refrigerated, tightly covered.

Mary's Canadian Cousin

In Canada, the Bloody Caesar, sometimes just shortened to Caesar, is to drinks what hockey is to sports; it's the bee's knees, the cat's meow, and every other superlative. But its birth is relatively recent development. In 1969 Walter Chell, who was restaurant manager at the Calgary Inn in Calgary, Alberta, was charged with creating a drink for the hotel's new Italian restaurant. He recalled eating pasta with clams in tomato sauce on a trip to Italy and decided it would work well for a drink, too. His original drink was made with puréed fresh clams. But fortuitously for the rest of the world Mott's introduced Clamato juice in the same year. While sales at first were slow, they skyrocketed after the company discovered Chell's drink, and by 1994 the company estimated that 70 percent of its Canadian sales were to make the drink.

Bottled Bloody Mary Mix to the Rescue

In the past decade the number of options for purchased Bloody Mary mix has grown from a few to a dizzying array, and there are opinions about each one of them. Some pack more heat than others, they vary in terms of their sweetness or tanginess, and then some are thicker than others to keep a pleasing thick texture when diluted by the liquor and ice.

There are even regional variations. Ones from the mid-Atlantic states feature blended spices like Old Bay, the dominant seasoning used when steaming prized Maryland blue crabs. South of the Mason-Dixon Line the local mixes frequently include barbecue sauce, and from Texas to the West Coast expect some Mexican flavors.

While this book is intended to encourage you to make your own basic mix or some variation on one, there are times when you have neither the time nor the ingredients around to let loose your inner master mixologist. To your rescue come good liquor stores, and, of course, the Internet.

I assembled a tasting panel and we tried bottled mixes in their virginal but chilled state right out of the bottle and then mixed them with a modest amount of vodka over ice. Here's a summary of those we really liked, all of which can be ordered online if not available in your region.

Dr. Swami & Bone Daddy's Spicy Cajun Bloody Mary Mix: In addition to all the basics of horseradish and Worcestershire there's a meaty richness to this mix from the inclusion of beef broth. The consistency is medium-thick so, once diluted with ice and liquor, it still keeps a solid texture.

Employees Only Bloody Mary Mix: Employees Only is a popular speakeasy bar in New York's Greenwich Village that has been glorifying the return to traditional cocktails since 2004. This mix delivers one of the most complex flavors among those we tried as well as the perfect consistency when mixed with liquor, although we thought it needed a bit of water added if intended as a juice only. It's one of the few we sampled that drew its briny flavor from crushed capers, and the horseradish tasted very fresh.

Master of Mixes Loaded Bloody Mary Mixer: There's no question that at less than $10 for a 1.75-liter bottle this mix wins hands down for value, and the flavor is great, too. With notes of horseradish and dill pickle, it also tastes very much like fresh vegetables because celery and cucumber are part of it. The texture is great right out of the bottle but becomes a bit thin for our taste once the drink is made.

Hoosier Momma Bloody Mary Maker: The scantily clad pinup holding a tomato on the label might not be the midwestern mother you envision, but this Hoosier Momma is full of flavor. Although the line extensions now include a spicy version and one made with sriracha, we found the original to be the best. Although mild on the verge of being sweet, it can easily be spiced up, but then you might not taste the hints of ginger and shiitake mushrooms. It's a chunky mix with big flecks of herbs and it dilutes well.

McClure's Pickles Bloody Mary Mix: The whole McClure family of Detroit started a pickle business using their grandmother's recipes about a decade ago, and now use a lot of the brine for a Bloody Mary mix. Vinegar is listed as the second ingredient, which indicates the flavor profile. You also get a good dose of dill and garlic, and the mix does thin down significantly upon adding ice.

Preservation & Co. Original Bloody Mary Mix: This product is made by a shop in Sacramento, California, and it creates a really complex drink. Some of the ingredients include tamarind, sriracha, capers, and Dijon mustard to balance the traditional lemon juice, Worcestershire, and horseradish. It had a very pleasing midrange consistency that was not overly thinned when transformed into a drink.

Ripe Bar Juice San Marzano Bloody Mary Mix: If you live in New England, California, or Arizona look for this mix made with luscious all-natural, non-GMO juice in the refrigerator case because it's a fresh product. Made by FreshBev Craft Juicery in New Haven, Connecticut, finding Ripe Bar Juice was as exciting as when we first saw bottles of orange juice and could eliminate cans of frozen concentrate from our grocery list forever. The company will ship to areas in which they don't have retail distribution.

Zing Zang Bloody Mary Mix: Zing Zang began about twenty years ago as a foodservice product for bars and restaurants, based on the personal recipe of the brand's owner, Richard Krohn. Its popularity led to the introduction of consumer sizes a few years later. This is a product for people who prefer V8 to tomato juice when making a mix from scratch. There's a prominent taste of celery seed but that is balanced by the garlic, chiles, and Worcestershire sauce. As bottled mixes go this one was not insanely high in sodium, and it's labeled as gluten-free.

Tempting the Tongue with a Salty Rim

While margarita glasses have been encrusted with a salted rim since the first mariachi sound track was recorded, it's only been in this century that Bloody Marys have been treated to a similar aesthetic enhancement: a rim of spiced salt crowning the glass.

Drinks are subjected to the "two G's" right before serving: garnish and garbage. In the former camp are all the ingredients added to enhance a drink's flavor or add some nutritional benefit. In the case of a Bloody Mary this is where everything from a celery stick to a wedge of lemon or lime or a skewer of olives comes in. Garbage is the category that includes paper umbrellas and swizzle sticks that add to the visual appeal of the presentation but serve no function. Rimming a glass falls somewhere between the two. Depending on the method used the salty mixture will either meld into the drink or it can be primarily decorative and bordering on annoying if it gets all over the fingers or makes a dark suit or dress look like you've spilled a snow cone.

Because the process involves inverting the glass, rimming obviously must be done before the drink is mixed, poured, or garnished. I suggest pouring in the actual Bloody Mary with a funnel to ensure that your careful rimming doesn't drip right into the drink.

How to Rim a Glass

There are two basic methods depending on whether you want to coat both sides of the rim or just one, or even part of one. Coating both sides of the rim definitely changes the flavor of the drink, while just rimming the outside or part of the outside keep it as a decorative element.

Cut a wedge of lemon or lime, depending on which juice you're using in the drink. Cut a slice vertically in the center of the wedge and insert the rim of the glass. Run it around the rim of the glass, twisting the glass in your hand. Place your salt mixture in a coffee saucer that has slightly sloping sides and place the glass upside down into the mixture. If you're a gadget freak, buy a two-level glass rimmer. One level has a sponge that you wet with lime juice or lemon juice, and the other level is a saucer for your salt.

If you just want to coat the outside rim of the glass, run the piece of citrus around the outside of the rim. Then hold the glass at an angle and roll the edge around in the seasoning mixture. Sometimes only two thirds of the glass is rimmed to allow sippers a respite from the salt mine.

Mixtures to Use for Rimming a Glass

A lot of the specific recipes in Chapters 4 and 5 of this book give a suggested formulation for the rimming salt, and you can always just use plain kosher salt or—for a change of pace—smoked salt. But there are other options in the supermarket spice section that will add complexity to the drink. Here are a few possibilities.

Old Bay: This mix was originally used to spice the prized blue crabs of the Chesapeake Bay. It contains mustard, paprika, celery salt, bay leaf, black pepper, crushed red pepper flakes, mace, cloves, allspice, nutmeg, cardamom, and ginger.

Cajun seasoning: First bottled in the 1980s and dubbed "blackening seasoning" by famed Cajun chef Paul Prudhomme, it's now available in every spice section. Some of the essential ingredients are paprika, salt, garlic powder, black pepper, onion powder, cayenne pepper, oregano, and thyme.

Tajin: Made in Jalisco, Mexico, this seasoning powder, called *salsa en polvo* in Spanish, is made from salt, dehydrated lime juice, and ground chiles. Introduced in 1985, in Mexico it's used on fruits and vegetables, too.

Grilling seasonings: Mixed herb-and-spice grilling rubs started out in the early 1990s when firms like Nantucket Off-Shore Seasonings introduced what is now the ubiquitous round metal can. The upscale rubs do not contain salt, so mix them with kosher salt in a ratio of one part rub to two parts salt. Then there are the mass-market blends produced by giants like McCormick. The Grill Mates varieties are excellent for rimming; I especially like the Roasted Garlic & Herb.

Bloody Mary Rim Mix

Here's the formulation of my favorite homemade rim mixture. It will only take a few minutes. It's a riff on Old Bay made from ingredients most of us have around.

Makes about ½ cup

¼ cup kosher salt
2 tablespoons sweet Spanish smoked paprika
(pimentón de la vera dulce)
2 tablespoons granulated garlic
1 tablespoon coarsely ground black pepper
2 teaspoons celery seeds
1 teaspoon dried thyme

Combine the salt, paprika, garlic, pepper, celery seed, and thyme in a container with a tight-fitting lid and shake well. Store in a dark, cool place for up to 4 months.

OLD BAY STARTED AS A SNEAKY TRICK

Gustav Brunn, a German immigrant living in Baltimore, formulated Old Bay in 1939. Back then steamed blue crabs were so plentiful in the Chesapeake Bay that they were given away free as bar snacks; at the same time caviar was a freebie in New York bars, where it was dubbed "Albany Beef." Brunn's bar-owner buddies wanted the crabs to be salty and spicy to encourage their customers to drink more beers so he concocted Old Bay, which is named for a passenger ship line that plied the waters of the Chesapeake Bay from Baltimore to Norfolk, Virginia, in the early twentieth century.

How to Become a Mixing Master

"Shaken, not stirred" was the quintessential description used to describe *the only* way a martini should be made by Ian Fleming's James Bond. There are a few hard-and-fast rules about drink mixing that are the equivalent of "never wear white after Labor Day." You should shake a drink if you want creaminess and stir a drink that you wish to remain clear. In Mr. Bond's case, the drink he sipped while immaculately dressed in black tie in between sessions of bedding double agents is technically termed a Bradford.

Shaking, the more aggressive form of mixing, aerates a drink and suspends air bubbles in it that add to its viscosity and create a cloudy appearance. It also is the more effective way to blend thick ingredients like cream or an egg white with liquor and thinner liquids.

Stirring is the preferred method for all drinks made only with ingredients containing alcohol. It keeps the liquor thicker and creates a smooth mouthfeel because less air is introduced. While bitters are not technically liquor, the small shake added to a Manhattan keeps it firmly on the list to be stirred.

But there's a third option. When mixing a Bloody Mary the best method of chilling it down and blending its myriad ingredients is neither to shake nor stir it. It should be "rolled."

The drink should be mixed in a large glass filled with ice and then poured into a second glass. This gentle transfer from one glass to another should continue until the drink is ideally chilled. The drink should then be strained into a clean glass filled with fresh ice before it is garnished.

But reality must eventually trump perfection. If you're mixing six or eight Bloody Marys at a time you're not going to roll them all individually from glass to glass. The best compromise is to stir, but gently. Pour the chilled mix over a pitcher full of ice cubes and stir with a long bar spoon (or a long cooking spoon if that's what you've got). You want a long spoon to fight the force of gravity and suspend any particles of ingredients like horseradish evenly through the mix.

Chilling with Sparkling Clear Ice Cubes

Except on the rare occasions that you want to serve your Bloody Mary straight up in a stemmed martini glass, you're going to use ice to chill it down and keep it cold. And there's nothing wrong with the cloudy ice that automatically spews out of an ice maker or forms in plastic trays.

But making clear ice is literally as easy as boiling water. There are all sorts of weird theories floating around the Internet on how to achieve clear ice cubes. But there's a really easy way and it works every time.

What makes ice cloudy are the minerals and trapped air in the tap water. You can start with distilled water or filter your tap water through a filtering pitcher.

The second part of the process to produce clear ice involves boiling the water twice. Bring it to a boil, allow it to cool until almost room temperature, and then bring it back to a boil.

At this point, go ahead and fill and freeze your ice cube trays. While the cubes may have a thin film on the top that appears cloudy, they will be much clearer than cubes made with water straight out of the tap.

Additions to Ice Cubes

Perhaps Gertrude Stein was correct that "a rose is a rose is a rose." But there's no reason why an ice cube can't add both an aesthetic touch as well as some additional flavor to a Bloody Mary.

If you want to float something inside the cubes, it's best to freeze them in two stages. Begin by filling the cups halfway and freezing the tray. Then add your ingredient, fill the cups to the top, and freeze it again. Here's a range of foods that look attractive in ice cubes: herb leaves such as cilantro, parsley, oregano, or basil; rings of jalapeño or serrano chiles; a twist of lemon or lime zest; a small olive, a pickled cocktail onion, or a few capers; or a few celery leaves.

Frosty and Flavorful Additions

While most ice cubes dilute the potency and texture of a Bloody Mary as they melt, cubes made with puréed vegetables, herbs, and spices actually alter the flavor of the drink.

One simple answer is to create ice cubes from your Bloody Mary mix. I started to do this after reading articles about serving iced tea with tea cubes and iced coffee with coffee cubes, either black or mixed with milk. As these cubes melt they just reinforce the flavors already in the glass. While ideal for those drinking a Virgin Mary (aka Bloody Shame) you can offer to add a little alcoholic refresher to drinks made with liquor.

Another trick is to make striped ice cubes by filling the tray half full with tomato juice spiked with horseradish and Worcestershire sauce. Once that layer freezes top it with a mixture of lemon and lime juice.

Then there are cubes that increase the complexity of the drink as they melt and dilute it. Here's one I make often.

Green Goddess Cubes

The combination of green ingredients that's then strained to freeze into these cubes changes the nature of the drink as you sip. Instead of diluting, the flavor of the drink keeps changing and sometimes intensifying.

Makes 1 tray

2 jalapeño or serrano chiles, seeds and ribs removed
1 large cucumber, halved and cut into ½-inch slices
3 small tomatillos, husked, rinsed, cored, and diced
1 garlic clove
2 tablespoons chopped fresh parsley
2 teaspoons anchovy paste

Combine the chiles, cucumber, tomatillos, garlic, parsley, and anchovy paste in a blender or food processor and purée until smooth. Force the mixture through a strainer, pressing with the back of a spoon to extract as much liquid as possible. Freeze the mixture in an ice cube tray until solid, then transfer the cubes to a heavy, resealable plastic bag.

Note: The cubes can be frozen for up to 6 months.

Choosing the Right Glass for a Bloody Mary

Just as there was a proper utensil assigned to eat every dish that was served at lavish Edwardian dinners like the ones dramatized in *Downton Abbey*, stocking a home bar with proper glassware also used to be carefully orchestrated by tradition. Every drink was assigned to a glass with a specific shape and capacity. (Back in the twentieth century folks had yet to be subjected to supersizing.)

But today Champagne and other sparkling wines are poured into tall flutes rather than wide coupe glasses, and the shape of the glass filled by a Bloody Mary varies as much as the flavorings mixed into the tomato juice.

The traditional glass was one in the "chimney glass" family, either the highball glass or the Collins glass. Both are straight-sided with flat bases and hold about twelve to fourteen ounces. Their differences: A highball glass is shorter and wider than a Collins glass; the Collins glass is usually served with a straw. The double old-fashioned glass has the same capacity, but its shape is short and squat. The double old-fashioned glasses typically have a thick base so that nonliquid ingredients can be crushed using a muddler before the liquids are poured in.

The twenty-ounce hurricane glass got its name because its curved shape is reminiscent of a hurricane lantern, not because it was popularized at Pat O'Brien's bar in the French Quarter of New Orleans, a city that has endured more than its share of hurricanes. Like many glasses used today for Bloody Marys, the hurricane glass flares out at the top, which allows for a skyscraper of garnishes.

Today you'll also see Bloody Marys served in traditional European beer glasses. The two most common are the pilsner glass and the weizen glass, both of which hold about sixteen ounces. The pilsner glass is tall and slender, and tapers outward from its footed base. Weizen glasses are also tall, but there's a serpentine curve to how they widen rather than the even sides of a pilsner.

A shape unrelated to these is the twelve-to-sixteen-ounce beer snifter, a brandy snifter on steroids popular in Europe for dark, aromatic beers. While the snifter shape doesn't allow for an elaborate garnish display, it does serve as a nice vessel to hold the drink.

Each recipe contains a drawing which is a recommendation for the best serving glass. You can always substitute whatever glass you have handy.

double old-fashioned

weizen beer

pilsner

stemmed martini

snifter

beer snifter

highball

collins

mason jar

CHAPTER 3

Variations
on the Classic

With the recipes in this chapter we begin to improvise on the classics. These drinks will feel familiar because they're all tomato based. But the remainder of their ingredients are drawn from cuisines around the world, from the sunny shores of Sicily and Provence to exotic heights of Asia. There are also some riffs on American regional cuisines, giving you plenty of ways to entice even those with a jaded palate.

Light Libation

Many Bloody Mary fans crave something a bit lighter during the summer months; they want the entire range of tastes but in a thinner matrix. That's why I developed this recipe. By straining the mix, you still have a vivid red juice full of rich and spicy flavors, but it's thin, which makes it easy to sip.

Makes 6 drinks

2 pounds ripe red tomatoes
2 garlic cloves
¼ small sweet onion, chopped
1 jalapeño or serrano chile, seeds and ribs removed, diced
1 to 2 tablespoons prepared white horseradish
2 teaspoons kosher salt
¼ cup freshly squeezed lemon juice
2 tablespoons celery bitters
3 tablespoons Old Bay seasoning for rimming the glasses (optional)
9 to 12 ounces vodka or Spicy Vodka (page 43)

SUGGESTED GARNISHES:
Strips of crispy thick-sliced bacon
Skewers of green olives alternated with cherry tomatoes and cocktail onions
Dilly Beans (page 149)
Lemon wedges

Place the tomatoes, garlic, onion, chile, horse-radish, and salt in a food processor or blender, and purée until smooth. Strain the liquid through a sieve, pressing with the back of a spoon to extract as much liquid as possible.

Combine the purée with the lemon juice and bitters in a pitcher and stir well. Chill well.

Rim 6 (12-ounce) glasses with Old Bay, if desired, following the instructions on pages 56–57.

Pour about 4 ounces (½ cup) of the mix into a pint glass, add 1½ to 2 ounces of the vodka, and fill the glass completely with ice. Roll the drink between 2 pint glasses to mix and chill for individual servings (see page 59), or pour the vodka and mix into a pitcher filled with ice and stir well with a long-handled spoon.

Strain the drink into a rimmed glass using a funnel to avoid wetting the rim. Add ice cubes, and garnish each drink with a strip or two of bacon; a skewer of olives, cherry tomatoes, and onions; a few dilly beans; and a lemon wedge. Serve immediately.

Note: The mix can be made up to 2 days in advance and refrigerated, tightly covered.

double old-fashioned

BAKED KALE CHIPS

We all know that kale is the prince of the produce department and about as close to nutritional nirvana as we're likely to get. But what I love most is how crispy it gets when baked, and a bowl these chips alongside Bloody Marys is a surefire winner.

Makes about 3 cups

1 pound curly kale, stems and large inner ribs removed
3 tablespoons olive oil
2 garlic cloves, minced
Salt and freshly ground black pepper

Preheat the oven to 350°F with the racks on the top and bottom rungs, and line 2 baking sheets with heavy-duty aluminum foil.

Rinse the kale and break it into bite-size pieces. Dry it using a salad spinner to remove as much moisture as possible. Place the kale in a large mixing bowl and toss it with the oil and garlic.

Arrange the kale on the prepared baking sheets and bake for 15 to 17 minutes, or until the kale is crisp. Reverse the position of the baking sheets midway through the baking.

Remove the pans from the oven and sprinkle the kale with salt and pepper to taste. Serve immediately.

Note: Any leftover chips should be stored at room temperature in a paper bag, and they should be eaten within a day.

Bloody Bull

The Bloody Bull is what you get when a Bloody Mary and a Bullshot (page 119) produce an offspring. It's recognizable as a basic Bloody Mary but the addition of beef consommé changes the nature of the drink. Most histories trace the bastard child to Brennan's in New Orleans in the mid 1950s, and the inclusion of some Guinness stout to increase the richness is a trick I observed at Brooklyn Star, a bar in Brooklyn, New York.

Makes 6 drinks

2¼ cups tomato juice

¾ cup double-strength beef consommé, such as Campbell's

½ cup strained tomatoes (passata di pomodoro)

½ cup Guinness stout beer

¼ cup freshly squeezed lemon juice

3 tablespoons dill pickle brine

2 tablespoons sambal oelek or sriracha sauce

1 tablespoon Worcestershire sauce

1 tablespoon prepared white horseradish

1 teaspoon celery seeds

3 tablespoons Creole seasoning for rimming the glasses (optional)

9 to 12 ounces vodka or Bacon-Infused Vodka (page 41)

SUGGESTED GARNISHES:

Dilly Beans (page 149)

Strips of Beef Jerky (page 153) or store-bought jerky

Lemon wedges

Combine the tomato juice, consommé, strained tomatoes, beer, lemon juice, brine, sambal oelek, Worcestershire sauce, horseradish, and celery seeds in a pitcher and stir well. Chill well.

Rim 6 (14-ounce) glasses with Creole seasoning, if desired, following the instructions on pages 56–57.

Pour about 6 ounces (¾ cup) of the mix into a pint glass, add 1½ to 2 ounces of the vodka, and fill the glass completely with ice. Roll the drink between 2 pint glasses to mix and chill for individual servings (see page 59), or pour the vodka and mix into a pitcher filled with ice and stir well with a long-handled spoon.

Strain the drink into a rimmed glass using a funnel to avoid wetting the rim. Add ice cubes, and garnish each drink with dilly beans, beef jerky, and lemon wedges. Serve immediately.

Note: The mix can be made up to 2 days in advance and refrigerated, tightly covered.

snifter

BARR FOOD

SCOTCH EGGS

Hard-cooked eggs in a crispy coat of herbed sausage could be either a garnish on a Bloody Mary or a snack to serve alongside the drink. They're a hearty addition to the repertoire of foods that go so well with the flavor profile of the drink.

Makes 1 dozen

EGGS:

8 large eggs, chilled, divided
1 pound bulk pork breakfast sausage
2 tablespoons chopped fresh parsley
2 tablespoons snipped fresh chives
1 tablespoon chopped fresh sage leaves
1½ teaspoons fresh thyme leaves
Cayenne pepper, as needed
2 tablespoons Dijon mustard
½ cup all-purpose flour
Salt and freshly ground black pepper
1½ cups plain dry breadcrumbs
Vegetable oil for frying

SAUCE:

½ cup mayonnaise
2 tablespoons Dijon mustard
2 tablespoons snipped fresh chives
2 tablespoons chopped fresh parsley
Freshly ground black pepper

Bring a large saucepan of water to a boil over high heat. Gently add 6 cold eggs, cover the pan, and bring the water back to a boil. Reduce the heat to low and simmer the eggs, uncovered, for 11 minutes. Plunge the hot eggs into a large mixing bowl of ice water, and let them cool in the water until chilled. Crack the shells all over against the sides of the mixing bowl, and then begin to peel them starting with the large end.

Combine the sausage, parsley, chives, sage, and thyme in a mixing bowl. Season with cayenne, and mix well with your hands. Beat the remaining 2 eggs with the mustard in a shallow bowl. Place the flour in a shallow bowl, and season with salt and black pepper. Place the breadcrumbs in another shallow bowl.

Dust the peeled eggs with the flour, then, using wet hands, pat one sixth of the sausage mixture around each egg. Dip the coated eggs into the egg mixture, and then roll them in the

recipe continues

Variations on the Classic ~ 73

breadcrumbs, pressing gently to get crumbs to adhere. Refrigerate the eggs for at least 30 minutes to allow the coating to adhere.

While the eggs chill, prepare the sauce. Combine the mayonnaise, mustard, chives, and parsley in a mixing bowl. Season with black pepper, and whisk well. Chill until ready to serve.

Heat 3 inches of oil in a deep-sided saucepan to 350°F. Add 3 eggs to the hot oil, and fry them, gently turning them occasionally with a slotted spoon, for 6 to 8 minutes, or until the eggs are dark brown and the sausage is cooked through. Remove the eggs from the pan with a slotted spoon, and drain well on paper towels. Repeat with the remaining eggs. When cool enough to handle, cut the eggs in half lengthwise. Serve hot, at room temperature, or chilled.

Note: The eggs can be prepared for frying up to 1 day in advance and refrigerated, tightly covered. If serving them cold, they can be fully cooked up to 2 days in advance, and refrigerated, tightly covered. If serving them hot, they can be fried up to 3 hours in advance and kept at room temperature. Reheat them in a 325°F oven for 5 minutes.

Variation: Substitute sweet or hot bulk Italian sausage for the breakfast sausage, and substitute 2 teaspoons Italian seasoning for the sage and thyme.

SCOTCH EGGS WERE BORN IN LONDON

Fortnum & Mason, the iconic London specialty store, claims to have invented Scotch eggs in 1738, and the earliest printed recipe dates to 1809. But the Scotch reference might not be to the land of kilts and lassies. Back then anchovies were often used in conjunction with meats, and those dishes were given the name Scotch. In addition to Scotch eggs, there's a dish called Scotch woodcock, which is scrambled eggs on toast with anchovies.

Ballpark Bloody

This drink got its name because the inclusion of mustard and relish in the Bloody Mary mix. A sausage garnish seemed like it would be right at home in a ballpark.

Makes 6 drinks

2 cups tomato juice

1 cup fire-roasted crushed tomatoes, such as Muir Glen or Pomì

⅓ cup sweet pickle relish

⅓ cup Dijon mustard

⅓ cup freshly squeezed lemon juice

1 tablespoon celery bitters

2 teaspoons ground cumin

1 teaspoon chili powder

¾ teaspoon dried oregano, preferably Mexican

Celery salt, as needed, plus 3 tablespoons for rimming the glasses (optional)

9 to 12 ounces vodka or Bacon-Infused Vodka (page 41)

SUGGESTED GARNISHES:

Skewers of grilled sausage, such as kielbasa or knackwurst

Skewers of cubed soft pretzels

Sweet and Tangy Pickles (page 146)

Lemon wedges

Combine the tomato juice, tomatoes, relish, mustard, lemon juice, bitters, cumin, chili powder, and oregano in a food processor or blender, and purée until smooth. Season with hot sauce and celery salt to taste. Chill well.

Rim 6 (14-ounce) glasses with celery salt, if desired, following the instructions on page 56–57.

Pour about 6 ounces (¾ cup) of the mix into a pint glass, add 1½ to 2 ounces of the vodka, and fill the glass completely with ice. Roll the drink between 2 pint glasses to mix and chill for individual servings (see page 59), or pour the vodka and mix into a pitcher filled with ice and stir well with a long-handled spoon.

Strain the drink into a rimmed glass using a funnel to avoid wetting the rim. Add ice cubes, and garnish each drink with a skewer of grilled sausage, a skewer of soft pretzel cubes, a pickle spear, and a lemon wedge. Serve immediately.

Notes: The mix can be made up to 2 days in advance and refrigerated, tightly covered.

Mexican oregano is widely available. It has a more pungent aroma and flavor than its Mediterranean cousin (both are in the mint family). If using Mediterranean oregano, increase the amount to 1 teaspoon to achieve the same flavor.

highball

WELSH RAREBIT GRILLED CHEESE

Bubbly cheese laced with mustard on crisp toast with strips of bacon and slices of tomato is classic "pub grub" in England, and its finger-food version is a great snack to accompany a Bloody Mary, too.

Makes 2 dozen pieces

1 pound sliced bacon
1 tablespoon unsalted butter
2 shallots, minced
½ cup Dijon mustard
24 slices white sandwich bread
7 ounces Cheddar cheese, thinly sliced
4 ripe plum tomatoes, cored, seeded, and thinly sliced
¾ cup mayonnaise

Preheat the oven to 400°F. Cover a rimmed baking sheet with heavy-duty aluminum foil, and place a wire rack on the foil. Arrange the strips of bacon on the rack, place the pan in the oven, and cook the bacon for 15 to 20 minutes, or until it becomes crisp and brown. Pat the bacon with paper towels, and set aside.

While the bacon cooks, heat the butter in a small skillet over medium heat. Add the shallots and cook for 5 minutes, or until soft and lightly browned. Stir the shallots into the mustard, and set aside.

To assemble the sandwiches, trim the crusts off of the bread using a serrated bread knife. Spread the mustard mixture on one side of 12 bread slices. Top the mustard with strips of bacon and then layers of cheese and tomato.

Cover your counter with parchment paper. Spread mayonnaise on one side of the remaining bread slices. Top the sandwiches with the mayonnaise side up and then flip the sandwiches over and spread mayonnaise on the other sides.

Heat a large griddle over medium heat. Grill the sandwiches for 3 to 4 minutes per side, or until brown and crusty. Allow them to cool for 3 minutes, and then cut them in half diagonally. Serve immediately.

Note: The sandwiches can be prepared up to 2 days in advance and refrigerated, tightly covered. Reheat them in a 375°F oven for 5 to 7 minutes, or until hot and crisp.

CELERY STUFFED WITH PIMIENTO CHEESE

Pimiento cheese is called "the pâté of the South," but its origins were in New York in the 1870s, which is when cream cheese was invented and pimiento peppers were first exported from Spain.

Makes 18 pieces

¾ cup shredded extra-sharp white Cheddar cheese

¾ cup shredded extra-sharp orange Cheddar cheese

½ cup mayonnaise

3 tablespoons cream cheese, at room temperature

1 tablespoon grated onion

1 garlic clove, pushed through a garlic press

¼ cup finely chopped pimientos, plus more for garnish

Salt and freshly ground black pepper

6 celery ribs

Combine the white Cheddar, orange Cheddar, mayonnaise, cream cheese, onion, and garlic in a food processor. Mix well, using on-and-off pulsing. Scrape the mixture into a mixing bowl.

Place the pimientos on a paper towel and pat them dry. Stir them into the cheese mixture, and season with salt and black pepper to taste.

Trim the wide end off each celery rib and trim the narrow end where it begins to branch; each rib should then be about 8 inches long. Cut a thin slice off the curved bottom of each rib so that it will sit flat and securely on a platter. Fill the center of the ribs with the cheese mixture, and garnish with additional chopped pimientos. Cut the ribs into 2- to 2½-inch lengths, and serve.

Note: The cheese mixture can be prepared up to 5 days in advance and refrigerated, tightly covered. Allow it to sit at room temperature for 30 minutes before spreading it.

Variations: Substitute Monterey Jack or jalapeño Jack for the white Cheddar cheese; reduce the pimientos to 2 tablespoons and add 2 tablespoons finely chopped green or black olives to the cheese mixture.

While celery is traditional, there are other fresh vegetables that can be embellished with the cheese mixture. Put a dollop at the wide end of a spear of Belgian endive, or cut 2-inch sections from an English cucumber and hollow out the center with a melon baller, or place some in the center of a leaf of radicchio.

Bowling Green Bloody

This is the perfect drink to accompany a rack of ribs or some pulled pork barbecue. It's got some sweetness to it and a bit of bourbon reinforces that Southern feel. Serve it in a pint-size Mason jar to complete the trip south of the Mason-Dixon Line.

Makes 6 drinks

2 garlic cloves
¼ cup diced red onion
2⅓ cups tomato juice, divided
⅓ cup barbecue sauce
3 tablespoons bourbon
2 tablespoons cider vinegar
2 tablespoons prepared white horseradish
2 tablespoons freshly squeezed lemon juice
2 tablespoons steak sauce
1 tablespoon Worcestershire sauce
1 tablespoon hot red pepper sauce, or more to taste
Salt and freshly ground black pepper
9 to 12 ounces Bacon-Infused Vodka (page 41) or plain vodka

GLASS RIM (OPTIONAL):
1 tablespoon kosher salt
1 tablespoon granulated sugar
1 tablespoon smoked Spanish paprika

SUGGESTED GARNISHES:
Strips of Bourbon-Maple Bacon (page 155) or regular bacon
Skewers of soft pretzel pieces alternated with cubes of Cheddar cheese
Celery sticks with leaves
Boiled shrimp

mason jar

Combine the garlic, onion, and ½ cup of the tomato juice in a food processor or blender. Purée until smooth.

Scrape the mixture into a pitcher and add the remaining tomato juice, barbecue sauce, bourbon, vinegar, horseradish, lemon juice, steak sauce, Worcestershire sauce, and hot red pepper sauce. Season with salt and black pepper to taste and stir well. Chill well.

Rim 6 (16-ounce) glasses with a combination of kosher salt, sugar, and smoked Spanish paprika, if desired, following the instructions on pages 56–57.

Pour about 6 ounces (¾ cup) of the mix into a pint glass, add 1½ to 2 ounces of the vodka, and fill the glass completely with ice. Roll the drink between 2 pint glasses to mix and chill for individual servings (see page 59), or pour the vodka and mix into a pitcher filled with ice and stir well with a long-handled spoon.

Strain the drink into a rimmed glass using a funnel to avoid wetting the rim. Add ice cubes, and garnish each drink with bacon strips, skewer of pretzels and cheese, a celery stick, and a shrimp resting on the rim of the glass. Serve immediately.

Note: The mix can be made up to 2 days in advance and refrigerated, tightly covered.

Gazpacho Mary

This riff on the famed Spanish soup was invented one day when I really wanted a Bloody Mary and was out of tomato juice, but I had some left-over gazpacho from a dinner the night before. While I instantly determined the olive oil should not be part of the drink, the puréed soup was a great mix. The garnishes keep the Spanish theme going.

Makes 6 drinks

2 cups tomato juice

½ cup strained tomatoes (passata di pomodoro)

¼ medium red onion, diced

½ cucumber, peeled and diced

½ red bell pepper, seeds and ribs removed, diced

2 large garlic cloves

1 jalapeño or serrano chile, seeds and ribs removed, diced

¼ cup balsamic vinegar

¼ cup freshly squeezed lime juice

1 to 2 tablespoons Harissa (page 30) or store-bought harissa, or more to taste

¼ cup chopped fresh cilantro

Salt and freshly ground black pepper

9 to 12 ounces vodka or Spicy Vodka (page 43)

GLASS RIM (OPTIONAL):

1½ tablespoons kosher salt

1½ tablespoons smoked Spanish paprika

SUGGESTED GARNISHES:

Boiled shrimp

Skewers of pitted Spanish olives alternated with cubes of Spanish ham or chorizo

Strips of red bell pepper

recipe continues

highball

Gazpacho Mary

Combine the tomato juice, strained tomatoes, onion, cucumber, bell pepper, garlic, chile pepper, vinegar, lime juice, and harrisa in a food processor or blender. Purée until smooth.

Strain half of the mixture through a fine sieve, pressing with the back of a spoon to extract as much liquid as possible. Stir the mixture into the unstrained half, stir in the cilantro, and season with salt and black pepper to taste. Chill well.

Rim 6 (14-ounce) glasses with a combination of kosher salt and smoked Spanish paprika, if desired, following the instructions on pages 56–57.

Pour 6 ounces (¾ cup) of the mix into a pint glass, add 1½ to 2 ounces of the vodka, and fill the glass completely with ice. Roll the drink between 2 pint glasses to mix and chill for individual servings (see page 59), or pour the vodka and mix into a pitcher filled with ice and stir well with a long-handled spoon.

Strain the drink into a rimmed glass using a funnel to avoid wetting the rim. Add ice cubes, and garnish each drink with a boiled shrimp draped over the edge of the glass, a skewer of olives and ham, and strips of bell pepper. Serve immediately.

Note: The mix can be made up to 2 days in advance and refrigerated, tightly covered.

SPANISH POTATO AND SAUSAGE TORTILLA

Many traditional Spanish tapas are great snacks to serve with Bloody Marys, and I'm especially fond of this thick omelet enlivened with spicy sausage because it's so good at room temperature, or even chilled, as well as hot. For a small group you can serve it in wedges, or spear cubes of it with toothpicks for a large crowd.

Makes 1 (10-inch diameter) tortilla

⅓ pound raw ground chorizo sausage
2 tablespoons olive oil
1 large onion, diced
2 garlic cloves, minced
8 ounces red potatoes, cut into ½-inch dice
8 large eggs
2 tablespoons whole milk
2 tablespoons chopped fresh parsley
Salt and freshly ground black pepper

Note: The dish can be prepared up to 2 days in advance and refrigerated, tightly covered.

Preheat the oven to 425°F.

Heat a 10-inch ovenproof skillet over medium-high heat. Add the sausage, and cook, stirring frequently, for 3 to 5 minutes, or until the sausage browns. Remove the sausage from the skillet with a slotted spoon, and set aside.

Discard the fat from the skillet, and heat the oil over medium-high heat. Add the onion and garlic, and cook, stirring frequently, for 3 minutes, or until the onion is translucent. Add the potatoes, cover the pan, and cook, stirring occasionally, for 10 to 12 minutes, or until the potatoes are tender.

While the potatoes cook, combine the eggs, milk, and parsley in a mixing bowl. Season with salt and pepper to taste, and whisk well. Reduce the heat to medium, return the sausage to the pan, and add the egg mixture. Cook for 4 minutes, or until the bottom of the omelet is lightly brown. Transfer the skillet to the oven, and bake for 10 to 15 minutes, or until the top is browned.

Run a spatula around the sides of the skillet and under the bottom of the omelet to release it. Slide the omelet gently onto a serving platter, and cut it into wedges or cubes. Serve hot, at room temperature, or chilled.

Muddled Masterpiece

Here's a drink for those who love the machinations of muddling to make drinks like a mojito. You get to mash down on tender cherry tomatoes, delicate basil leaves, and rugged lime wedges before putting in the mix and liquor.

Makes 6 drinks

2 cups tomato juice

¼ cup Pickapeppa Sauce, or more to taste

2 tablespoons Worcestershire sauce

Salt and freshly ground black pepper

3 tablespoons Creole seasoning for rimming the glasses (optional)

24 red cherry tomatoes

2 limes, cut into 6 wedges each

½ cup firmly packed fresh basil leaves

9 to 12 ounces vodka

SUGGESTED GARNISHES:

Lime wedges

Skewers of cherry tomatoes alternated with small balls of fresh mozzarella and folded basil leaves

Skewers of grilled Italian sausage or salami cubes

Sweet and Tangy Pickles (page 146)

Combine the tomato juice, Pickapeppa Sauce, and Worcestershire sauce in a pitcher. Season with salt and black pepper to taste, and stir well. Chill well.

Rim 6 (12-ounce) glasses with Creole seasoning, if desired, following the instructions on page 56–57.

Place 4 cherry tomatoes, 2 lime wedges, and some basil leaves in each glass. Use a cocktail muddler to crush the ingredients.

Pour about 4 ounces (½ cup) of the mix into a pint glass, add 1½ to 2 ounces of the vodka, and fill the glass completely with ice. Roll the drink between 2 pint glasses to mix and chill for individual servings (see page 59), or pour the vodka and mix into a pitcher filled with ice and stir well with a long-handled spoon.

Strain the drink into a rimmed glass using a funnel to avoid wetting the rim. Add ice cubes, and garnish the drink with a lime wedge; a skewer of cherry tomatoes, fresh mozzarella, and basil leaves; a skewer of grilled sausage; and a pickle spear. Serve immediately.

Note: The mix can be made up to 2 days in advance and refrigerated, tightly covered.

double old-fashioned

PARMESAN SHALLOT FINGERS

Sweet shallots and sharp mustard are flavor accents to the creamy cheese topping on these toasts that pair so well with any tomato-based Bloody Mary. And since they freeze so well you can keep them on hand for impromptu gatherings. While I usually serve these as a snack, they can be woven onto a skewer to use as a garnish, too.

Makes 2 dozen pieces

2 tablespoons unsalted butter
2 large shallots, minced
12 slices white sandwich bread
Salt and freshly ground black pepper
¼ cup Dijon mustard
½ cup mayonnaise
¾ cup freshly grated Parmesan cheese

Note: The slices can be made up to 2 days in advance and refrigerated, tightly covered; they can also be frozen for up to 2 months. Reheat chilled slices in a 350°F oven for 5 to 7 minutes and frozen slices for 10 to 12 minutes.

Preheat the broiler, and cover a baking sheet with heavy-duty aluminum foil.

Heat the butter in a small skillet over medium-high heat. Add the shallots and cook, stirring frequently, for 5 to 7 minutes, or until the shallots soften and are lightly browned. Season with salt and pepper to taste, and scrape the shallots into a mixing bowl.

Trim the crusts off the bread slices using a serrated bread knife and cut each slice in half. Arrange the slices on the baking sheet. Broil the bread 8 inches from the broiler element for 30 seconds to 1 minute, or until toasted. Remove the bread from the oven.

Turn the bread slices over and spread mustard on the untoasted side. Add the mayonnaise and cheese to the mixing bowl with the shallots, season with salt and pepper to taste, and stir well.

Spread 1 scant tablespoon of the mixture on top of the mustard on each bread slice. Broil the slices for 1 to 2 minutes, or until the tops are brown and bubbly. Watch them carefully as they broil. Serve immediately.

Bloody Maja

Aquavit is the leading spirit in the Scandinavian countries, and like vodka it's distilled most often from potatoes or grain. But unlike vodka it is always flavored, with caraway and dill being the primary spices, although some brands also include cumin and fennel. The fresh dill in this libation plays beautifully off the spices in the base.

Makes 6 drinks

1 teaspoon fennel seeds

1 teaspoon caraway seeds

2½ cups tomato juice

¼ cup freshly squeezed lemon juice

2 tablespoons prepared white horseradish

1 tablespoon celery bitters

⅓ cup finely chopped fresh dill

Salt and freshly ground black pepper

3 tablespoons celery salt for rimming the glasses (optional)

9 to 12 ounces aquavit

SUGGESTED GARNISHES:

Fennel stalks with fronds attached

Skewers with pinwheels of gravlax or smoked salmon

Lemon wedges

Place the fennel seeds and caraway seeds in a small, dry skillet and toast them for 2 minutes, or until fragrant and turning brown. Crush the seeds in a spice grinder, in a pepper grinder, or with a mortar and pestle.

Combine the ground seeds, tomato juice, lemon juice, horseradish, celery bitters, and dill in a pitcher and stir well. Season with salt and pepper to taste, and chill well.

Rim 6 (12-ounce) glasses with celery salt, if desired, following the instructions on page 56–57.

Pour 4 ounces (½ cup) of the mix into a pint glass, add 1½ to 2 ounces of the aquavit, and fill the glass completely with ice. Roll the drink between 2 pint glasses to mix and chill for individual servings (see page 59), or pour the aquavit and mix into a pitcher filled with ice and stir well with a long-handled spoon.

Strain the drink into a rimmed glass using a funnel to avoid wetting the rim. Add ice cubes, and garnish each drink with a fennel stalk and a skewer of gravlax and rest a lemon wedge on the rim of the glass. Serve immediately.

Note: The mix can be made up to 2 days in advance and refrigerated, tightly covered.

highball

SMOKED SALMON SPREAD

This spread has a blushing pink color and an almost addictive flavor. It blends delicate fresh salmon with flecks of vibrant smoked salmon in a cream cheese matrix enlivened with horseradish, scallions, and dill. For a fancy presentation you can pipe it onto toast points or cucumber slices with a pastry bag, or just put it out with a basket of breads and crackers.

Makes 3 cups

8 ounces salmon fillet

2 teaspoons Old Bay seasoning

2 (8-ounce) packages cream cheese, at room temperature

3 tablespoons freshly squeezed lemon juice

2 tablespoons prepared white horseradish

4 ounces smoked salmon, finely chopped

3 scallions, white parts and 4 inches of green tops, chopped

3 tablespoons chopped fresh dill

Freshly ground black pepper

Sprinkle the salmon fillet with the Old Bay and place it in a microwave-safe dish. Cover the dish with plastic wrap and microwave the fish on high for 3 minutes. Allow the fish to sit covered for 2 minutes, then remove the plastic and refrigerate the salmon until cold. Remove and discard the skin, and break the salmon into 1-inch chunks.

Place the cooked salmon, cream cheese, lemon juice, and horseradish in a food processor. Purée until smooth. Scrape the mixture into a mixing bowl and stir in the smoked salmon, scallion, and dill. Season with pepper to taste and refrigerate until well chilled.

Note: The spread can be made 2 days in advance and refrigerated, tightly covered.

Sicilian Sipper

Here's a drink for all lovers of lusty Italian food. It's got tomatoes in two forms—juice plus the long-simmered taste of marinara sauce. I think of this as a winter drink, and it goes beautifully with pizza and pasta.

Makes 6 drinks

3 garlic cloves

¼ cup firmly packed fresh basil leaves

2 tablespoons firmly packed fresh oregano leaves

½ to 1½ teaspoons crushed red pepper flakes, or more to taste

¾ cup marinara sauce

3 cups tomato juice

⅓ cup red wine vinegar

2 tablespoons freshly squeezed lemon juice

Salt and freshly ground black pepper

9 to 12 ounces vodka or Spicy Vodka (page 43)

GLASS RIM (OPTIONAL):

2 tablespoons kosher salt

1 tablespoon Italian seasoning

SUGGESTED GARNISHES:

Fresh fennel stalks with fronds attached

Herbed Parmesan Crisps (page 157)

Skewers of cherry tomatoes alternated with small balls of fresh mozzarella and folded fresh basil leaves

Lemon wedges

Place the garlic, basil, oregano, crushed red pepper flakes, and marinara sauce in a food processor or blender, and purée until smooth. Strain the liquid through a sieve, pressing with the back of a spoon to extract as much liquid as possible.

Combine the purée, tomato juice, vinegar, and lemon juice in a pitcher. Season with salt and black pepper to taste, and stir well. Chill well.

Rim 6 (16-ounce) glasses with a combination of kosher salt and Italian seasoning, if desired, following the instructions on page 56–57.

Pour about 6 ounces (¾ cup) of the mix into a pint glass, add 1½ to 2 ounces of the vodka, and fill the glass completely with ice. Roll the drink between 2 pint glasses to mix and chill for individual servings (see page 59), or pour the vodka and mix into a pitcher filled with ice and stir well with a long-handled spoon.

Strain the drink into a rimmed glass using a funnel to avoid wetting the rim. Add ice cubes, and garnish each drink with fennel stalks; Parmesan crisps; skewers of cherry tomatoes, fresh mozzarella, and basil leaves; and lemon wedges. Serve immediately.

pilsner

BAKED SHRIMP SCAMPI ROLLS

Keeping to the rule that the snacks served with your Bloody Mary should always be finger food, here is a handheld version of shrimp scampi that delivers all the herb-and-garlic goodness of the dish. The pieces can be skewered as a garnish as well as served as a snack.

Makes 3 dozen pieces

Vegetable oil spray
12 slices white sandwich bread
12 ounces raw shrimp, peeled and deveined
3 garlic cloves, sliced
1 large egg white
2 tablespoons cornstarch
1 tablespoon olive oil
1 tablespoon dry white wine
2 scallions, white parts and 3 inches of green tops,
    cut into 1-inch sections
2 tablespoons fresh parsley leaves
1 tablespoon fresh oregano leaves
Salt and freshly ground black pepper

Preheat the oven to 425°F. Cover a baking sheet with heavy-duty aluminum foil and coat the foil with vegetable oil spray.

Remove the crusts from the bread slices using a serrated bread knife. Roll each slice with a rolling pin until the bread slice is thin but still pliable.

Combine the shrimp, garlic, egg white, cornstarch, olive oil, and wine in a food processor. Purée until smooth, stopping a few times to scrape the sides of the work bowl. Add the scallions, parsley, and oregano and chop them finely, using on-and-off pulsing. Scrape the mixture into a mixing bowl and season with salt and pepper to taste.

Lay the bread slices out on a counter and place 1 heaping tablespoon of filling in a line down the long side of each slice. Roll the bread around the filling so that the edges meet, and place the rolls, seam-side down, on the prepared baking sheet. Spray the tops with vegetable oil spray.

Bake the rolls for 5 minutes, turn them over, and bake for 3 minutes more, or until browned. Cut each into 3 sections with a serrated knife, and serve immediately.

Notes: The filling can be prepared 1 day in advance and refrigerated, tightly covered. Fill the bread and bake the rolls just before serving.

If you don't have a rolling pin, or you're using it to prop open a window, you can use a clean wine or soda bottle to roll out the bread slices.

Mediterranean Magic

Clear and bright flavors are characteristic of the sunny cuisine of Provence, and that's what you'll find in this drink. Everything from olives to oranges to herbs are part of the mix. Taking a sip will transport you to a terrace overlooking the deep blue sea.

Makes 6 drinks

3 tablespoons prepared black olive tapenade

2 garlic cloves

Peeled zest from ½ orange

2 tablespoons chopped fresh basil leaves

2 tablespoons Harissa (page 30) or store-bought harissa, or more to taste

1 tablespoon fresh oregano leaves

1 tablespoon fresh rosemary leaves

1 tablespoon anchovy paste, or 2 teaspoons kosher salt

1 teaspoon celery seeds

3 cups tomato juice, divided

½ cup freshly squeezed orange juice

⅓ cup freshly squeezed lemon juice

2 teaspoons orange bitters

Freshly ground black pepper

9 to 12 ounces vodka or Citrus Vodka (page 42)

6 ounces dry sherry

GLASS RIM (OPTIONAL):

2 tablespoons kosher salt

1 tablespoon herbes de Provence

SUGGESTED GARNISHES:

Stalks of fennel with fronds attached

Lemon wedges

Sprigs of fresh rosemary

Boiled shrimp

Toothpicks of oil-cured Provençal olives

weizen beer

Place the tapenade, garlic, orange zest, basil, harissa, oregano, rosemary, anchovy paste, celery seeds, and 1 cup of the tomato juice in a food processor or blender, and purée until smooth. Strain the liquid through a sieve, pressing with the back of a spoon to extract as much liquid as possible.

Combine the strained purée and the remaining tomato juice with the orange juice, lemon juice, and orange bitters in a pitcher and stir well. Season with pepper to taste, and chill well.

Rim 6 (16-ounce) glasses with a combination of kosher salt and herbes de Provence, if desired, following the instructions on page 56–57.

Pour about 6 ounces (¾ cup) of the mix into a pint glass, add 1½ to 2 ounces of the vodka and 1 ounce of the sherry, and fill the glass completely with ice. Roll the drink between 2 pint glasses to mix and chill for individual servings (see page 59), or pour the vodka and sherry and mix into a pitcher filled with ice and stir well with a long-handled spoon.

Strain the drink into a rimmed glass using a funnel to avoid wetting the rim. Add ice cubes, and garnish each drink with a fennel stalk, lemon wedge, rosemary sprig, boiled shrimp, and toothpick of olives. Serve immediately.

Note: The mix can be made up to 2 days in advance and refrigerated, tightly covered.

Marie du Jardin

If you leave out the vodka, this aromatic and delicious cooked vegetable base could easily be served as a soup, too. The color is vibrant and the herbs enliven it even further.

Makes 6 drinks

1 pound ripe red tomatoes, cored and diced
½ small carrot, diced
½ celery rib, sliced
¼ red bell pepper, seeds and ribs removed, diced
¼ small beet, thinly sliced
3 garlic cloves
½ cup diced red onion
½ cup firmly packed fresh spinach leaves
2 tablespoons fresh parsley
1 tablespoon fresh thyme leaves
1 tablespoon fresh rosemary leaves
2 to 3 tablespoons Harissa (page 30) or store-bought harissa
1 tablespoon anchovy paste
¼ cup red wine vinegar
¼ cup freshly squeezed lemon juice
Salt and freshly ground black pepper
9 to 12 ounces vodka

GLASS RIM (OPTIONAL):
2 tablespoons kosher salt
1 tablespoon herbes de Provence

SUGGESTED GARNISHES:
Lemon wedges
Dilly Beans (page 149)
Skewer of cornichons alternated with black niçoise olives
Herbed Parmesan Crisps (page 157) or breadsticks

snifter

Combine the tomatoes, carrot, celery, bell pepper, beet, garlic, onion, spinach, parsley, thyme, rosemary, harissa, anchovy paste, and ¾ cup of water in a saucepan and bring to a boil over medium-high heat. Reduce the heat to low, cover the pan, and simmer the mixture for 15 to 20 minutes, or until the vegetables are all tender.

Allow the mixture to cool for 10 minutes. Purée it with an immersion blender or transfer it to a blender and purée. Strain half of the mixture through a fine sieve, pressing with the back of a spoon to extract as much liquid as possible. Stir into the unstrained half and add in the vinegar and lemon juice. Season with salt and black pepper to taste. Chill well.

Rim 6 (14-ounce) glasses with a combination of kosher salt and herbes de Provence, if desired, following the instructions on page 56–57.

Pour about 6 ounces (¾ cup) of the mix into a pint glass, add 1½ to 2 ounces of the vodka, and fill the glass completely with ice. Roll the drink between 2 pint glasses to mix and chill for individual servings (see page 59), or pour the vodka and mix into a pitcher filled with ice and stir well with a long-handled spoon.

Strain the drink into a rimmed glass using a funnel to avoid wetting the rim. Add ice cubes, and garnish each drink with a lemon wedge, dilly beans, a skewer of cornichon and olives, and a Parmesan crisp. Serve immediately.

Note: The mix can be made up to 2 days in advance and refrigerated, tightly covered.

Asian Adventure

There are ingredients in this drink drawn from a number of Asian cuisines, such as gochujang from Korea, wasabi from Japan, and vinegar from China. All of these flavors hit the same notes as more traditional Bloody Mary ingredients: peppery, spicy, and sour.

Makes 6 drinks

2 cups tomato juice

⅔ cup strained tomatoes (passata di pomodoro)

2 scallions, white parts and 4 inches of green tops, cut into ¾-inch pieces

2 garlic cloves

3 tablespoons soy sauce

3 tablespoons Chinese black vinegar

2 tablespoons gochujang or sriracha sauce, or more to taste

1 to 2 teaspoons wasabi powder, or more to taste

1½ teaspoons toasted sesame oil

2 tablespoons chopped fresh cilantro

Salt and freshly ground black pepper

9 to 12 ounces vodka or Spicy Vodka (page 43)

GLASS RIM (OPTIONAL):

2½ tablespoons kosher salt

1 teaspoon wasabi powder

SUGGESTED GARNISHES:

Scallions

Stalks of baby bok choy

Skewers of sushi

Gingered Carrot Pickles (page 147)

Combine the tomato juice, strained tomatoes, scallions, garlic, soy sauce, vinegar, gochujang, wasabi, and oil in a food processor or blender. Purée until smooth. Stir in the cilantro, and season with salt and pepper to taste. Chill well.

Rim 6 (14-ounce) glasses with a combination of salt and wasabi, if desired, following the instructions on page 56–57.

Pour about 6 ounces (¾ cup) of the mix into a pint glass, add 1½ to 2 ounces of the vodka, and fill the glass completely with ice. Roll the drink between 2 pint glasses to mix and chill for individual servings (see page 59), or pour the vodka and mix into a pitcher filled with ice and stir well with a long-handled spoon.

Strain the drink into a rimmed glass using a funnel to avoid wetting the rim. Add ice cubes, and garnish each drink with a scallion, a stalk of baby bok choy, a few pieces of sushi on a skewer, and a carrot pickle spear. Serve immediately.

Note: The mix can be made up to 2 days in advance and refrigerated, tightly covered.

highball

Asian Adventures with Tuna Poke
with Mango and Avacado (page 98)

TUNA POKE WITH MANGO AND AVOCADO

More and more people are saying sayonara to sashimi and ta-ta to tuna tartare. For those in the know, the way to enjoy raw fish now hails from Hawaii, and it's called poke (pronounced *POH-kay* to rhyme with "okay"). You can serve poke as a snack on rice crackers, slices of cucumber, or endive or Bibb lettuce leaves, or by itself in porcelain Asian soupspoons.

Makes 8 to 12 servings

2 tablespoons white sesame seeds

3 scallions, white parts and 4 inches of green tops

1 tablespoon grated fresh ginger

¼ cup soy sauce

2 tablespoons toasted sesame oil

½ small jalapeño or serrano chile, seeds and ribs removed, finely chopped (optional)

1 ripe avocado, peeled and cut into ½-inch dice

2 tablespoons freshly squeezed lime juice

1 ripe yellow Champagne (Ataulfo) mango or ½ Tommy Atkins mango, cut into ½-inch dice

1 pound sushi-grade tuna or salmon, cut into ½-inch cubes

3 tablespoons chopped fresh cilantro

Salt and freshly ground black pepper

Seaweed salad for serving (optional)

Place a small skillet over medium heat and toast the sesame seeds for 3 minutes, or until browned. Set aside. Chop the white parts of the scallions and thinly slice the green tops on the diagonal. Reserve them separately.

Combine 1 tablespoon of the sesame seeds, chopped white scallions, ginger, soy sauce, oil, and chile, if using, in a mixing bowl and stir well. Toss the avocado with the lime juice, and add it to the bowl along with the mango, tuna, and cilantro. Toss gently, and season with salt and black pepper to taste.

To serve, place a mound of the fish mixture on a small plate, and garnish with the remaining sesame seeds and seaweed salad, if using.

Notes: The dish can be made up to 1 hour in advance and refrigerated, with plastic wrap pressed onto the surface to keep the avocado from discoloring.

There are two main species of mangoes in our markets. Champagne, sometimes called Ataulfo mangoes, are small, have yellow skin, and are almost flat in shape. The Tommy Atkins mango is rounder and about twice the size, and its peel is a reddish color with green and orange accents.

BLACK OLIVE AND RAISIN TAPENADE

Tapenade is a classic Provençal spread, and I love this version because the saltiness of the olives is balanced by the sweetness of brandy-soaked raisins. Serve it with pita crisps or crackers.

Makes 2 cups

¾ cup raisins
¼ cup brandy
1½ cups pitted oil-cured black olives
2 garlic cloves, minced
3 tablespoons freshly squeezed lemon juice
1 tablespoon anchovy paste, or ½ teaspoon salt
1 tablespoon chopped fresh parsley
1 teaspoon fresh thyme leaves
⅔ cup olive oil
2 tablespoons capers, drained and rinsed
Freshly ground black pepper

Combine the raisins and brandy in a small microwave-safe bowl, and microwave on high for 1 minute.

Combine the raisin mixture, olives, garlic, lemon juice, anchovy paste, parsley, and thyme in a food processor. Purée until smooth. Add the oil slowly through the feed tube, and mix well.

Scrape the mixture into a mixing bowl, and stir in the capers. Season with pepper to taste.

Note: The spread can be made up to 2 days in advance and refrigerated, tightly covered. Allow it to reach room temperature before serving.

Variation: Substitute dried figs or dates for the raisins.

GINGER GRAVLAX WITH CILANTRO MUSTARD SAUCE

Traditional gravlax is a Scandinavian dish; it literally means "buried fish." The basic combination of salt and sugar—the curing agents—are part of this recipe, however the classic dill has been replaced by pungent ginger. The Asian theme is reinforced with aromatic sesame oil and cilantro in the mustard sauce. This is not an impromptu dish, however. Please note that it must be started two days in advance.

Makes 3 dozen canapés

GRAVLAX:
1½ pounds skin-on salmon fillet
1 cup granulated sugar
1 cup kosher salt
¼ cup ground ginger
¼ cup coarsely ground black pepper
1 thin baguette, thinly sliced and toasted, or melba
   toast crackers
Sprigs of fresh cilantro

CILANTRO MUSTARD SAUCE:
½ cup Dijon mustard
⅓ cup honey
¼ cup toasted sesame oil
¼ cup chopped fresh cilantro

Rinse the salmon fillet under cold water and rub your hand across the surface from the tail to the head end. Remove any small bones with tweezers. Combine the sugar, salt, ginger, and pepper. Place one third of the mixture in the bottom of a glass baking dish. Place the salmon on top, skin-side down, and then spread on the remaining seasoning mixture.

Cover the baking dish with a double layer of plastic wrap and place a smaller baking dish over the fillet. Weight the salmon down with 5 pounds of cans or a heavy skillet for 3 hours at room temperature. Pour off any liquid that has accumulated and transfer the weighted salmon to the refrigerator for 2 days.

For the sauce, whisk together the mustard, honey, oil, and cilantro until smooth. Refrigerate the sauce, tightly covered.

To serve, rinse the coating off the salmon. Cut the fish on the diagonal into very thin slices, starting at the tail end of the fillet. Form the slices into small circles and place each on a toasted bread slice or cracker. Spoon a dab of sauce into the center of the circle and garnish with a few leaves of cilantro.

Note: The salmon can be sliced up to 1 day in advance. Do not arrange it until just before serving.

Variation: For traditional gravlax, substitute ⅔ cup chopped fresh dill for the ground ginger and add 1 tablespoon fennel seeds to the curing mix. For the sauce, substitute olive oil for the sesame oil, chopped fresh dill for the cilantro, and 2 tablespoons granulated sugar for the honey.

Korean Cocktail

Spicy and tangy kimchi, the national food of Korea, contains all the assertive flavors associated with a Bloody Mary right in one food, and once it's puréed it becomes almost a "convenience food" to make a great drink. And with all the health benefits associated with eating fermented foods, you're doing your body a favor.

Makes 6 drinks

1 cup kimchi

3 cups tomato juice

2 tablespoons freshly squeezed lemon juice

1 tablespoon Thai fish sauce (nam pla)

2 teaspoons orange bitters

9 to 12 ounces vodka or Spicy Vodka (page 43)

GLASS RIM (OPTIONAL):

2½ tablespoons kosher salt

2 teaspoons Korean red pepper flakes (gochugaru)

SUGGESTED GARNISHES:

Stalks of baby bok choy

Skewers of boiled shrimp

Gingered Carrot Pickles (page 147)

Lemon wedges

Place the kimchi in a food processor or blender, and purée until smooth. Strain the liquid through a sieve, pressing with the back of a spoon to extract as much liquid as possible.

Combine the kimchi purée, tomato juice, lemon juice, fish sauce, and orange bitters in a pitcher, and stir well. Chill well.

Rim 6 (14-ounce) glasses with a combination of salt and Korean red pepper flakes, if desired, following the instructions on page 56–57.

Pour about 6 ounces (¾ cup) of the mix into a pint glass, add 1½ to 2 ounces of the vodka, and fill the glass completely with ice. Roll the drink between 2 pint glasses to mix and chill for individual servings (see page 59), or pour the vodka and mix into a pitcher filled with ice and stir well with a long-handled spoon.

Strain the drink into a rimmed glass using a funnel to avoid wetting the rim. Add ice cubes, and garnish each drink with baby bok choy, a skewer of boiled shrimp, and carrot pickle spears, and rest a lemon wedge on the rim of the glass. Serve immediately.

Note: The mix can be made up to 2 days in advance and refrigerated, tightly covered.

highball

Sake to Me

Any visitor to a sushi bar knows that the flavors of wasabi, soy sauce, and pickled ginger blend well, and they really enhance tomato juice in this light and refreshing drink spiked with Japanese sake.

Makes 6 drinks

2½ cups tomato juice
½ cup strained tomatoes (passata di pomodoro)
1 to 2 teaspoons wasabi powder, or more to taste
2 tablespoons shoyu or reduced-sodium soy sauce
2 tablespoons liquid from pickled ginger
2 tablespoons unseasoned rice vinegar
18 ounces (2¼ cups) junmai sake

GLASS RIM (OPTIONAL):
2½ tablespoons kosher salt
½ teaspoon wasabi powder

SUGGESTED GARNISHES:
Scallions
Skewers of sushi
Skewers of cubed Asian Sesame Pickles (page 148)
   alternated with folded pieces of pickled ginger

Combine the tomato juice, strained tomatoes, wasabi, shoyu, pickled ginger liquid, and vinegar in a pitcher and stir well to dissolve the wasabi powder. Chill well.

Rim 6 (12-ounce) glasses with a combination of salt and wasabi, if desired, following the instructions on page 56–57.

Pour about 6 ounces (¾ cup) of the mix into a pint glass, add 3 ounces of the sake, and fill the glass completely with ice. Roll the drink between 2 pint glasses to mix and chill for individual servings (see page 59), or pour the sake and mix into a pitcher filled with ice and stir well with a long-handled spoon.

Strain the drink into a rimmed glass using a funnel to avoid wetting the rim. Add ice cubes, and garnish each drink with a scallion, a skewer of sushi, and a skewer of pickles and pickled ginger. Serve immediately.

Note: The mix can be made up to 2 days in advance and refrigerated, tightly covered.

double old-fashioned

CHAPTER 4

Contemporary Concoctions

This chapter is where you'll look for drinks when you're feeling adventurous— when you want a drink that has all the flavor elements you love in a Bloody Mary but doesn't look like a Bloody Mary.

While there are tomatoes—or their first cousins named tomatillos—in some of these drinks, the drinks themselves can be yellow, green, or even clear. There's a lot of spices in many of them, but the heat is balanced by the sweetness of fresh fruits.

There are also many recipes in this chapter than use South American spirits instead of vodka. As I said, these are the drinks to try when you're feeling adventurous.

Spirits from the Southern Hemisphere

If you've sipped on a margarita you're already acquainted with one of the main Latin American forms of liquor—tequila. But farther down in South America, there are equally delicious distilled spirits that are just gaining popularity in this country.

But there might be some things you don't know about tequila; it is as dependent on terroir as a wine grape. Tequila is distilled from blue agave plants that grow in the red volcanic soil of the Mexican state of Jalisco. Those grown in the mountain highlands are larger and sweeter than those from the lowlands, which have a more herbaceous aroma and flavor. To be sold in the United States tequila must be at least 40 percent alcohol (80 proof), but that's higher than the level distilled for consumption in Mexico.

In Brazil it's sugarcane juice that serves as the base for cachaça, the country's national liquor and the basis for the lime-flavored Caipirinha cocktail. The Portuguese switched the lucrative sugar-production business from the islands of Madeira to Brazil in the mid-sixteenth century. Almost all the cachaça produced never leaves Brazil.

Like rum, cachaça comes both clear and amber in color. The clear is usually less expensive because it hasn't been aged, but some of the finer ones are aged for at least a year to give them a smoother finish.

The comparisons are frequently made between rum and cachaça because sugarcane is the base for both. The major difference is that rum is most often distilled from molasses, a by-product that results after the refineries have boiled the cane juice to extract the most sugar crystals possible. On the other hand, cachaça is made from sugarcane juice that is fermented and distilled for the purpose of making the spirit.

And then there's pisco. Pisco was new to me on my first trip to Chile in 2013, but I'm now delighted to say it's for sale in most liquor stores. It's a great addition to many drinks above and beyond the pisco sours touted in its native lands.

Pisco is made in both Chile and Peru and it's a clear or light amber-colored brandy made by distilling wine pressed from grapes into a high-proof spirit; Chile's production is about three times the volume of Peru's because the country has such rich grape-growing regions. Of these South American spirits, pisco comes the closest to adding alcohol with little flavor to drinks, sort of like vodka.

Clear Sailing

While getting the tomato mixture to become perfectly clear takes a bit of time, it's not labor intensive nor does it involve alchemy. People taking their first sip have no idea what to expect, and then they discover that what looks like a martini is really a delicious Bloody Mary.

Makes 6 drinks

1 pound ripe tomatoes (they can be any color), diced
1 garlic clove
1 small shallot, chopped
¼ jalapeño or serrano chile, seeds and ribs removed
2 teaspoons kosher salt
1 tablespoon celery bitters
1 tablespoon Thai fish sauce (nam pla)
3 tablespoons celery salt for rimming the glasses (optional)
9 to 12 ounces vodka

SUGGESTED GARNISHES:
Toothpick with multicolored cherry tomatoes
Boiled shrimp

Combine the tomatoes, garlic, shallot, chile, and salt in a food processor or blender. Chop the mixture finely using on-and-off pulsing. Transfer the mixture to a heavy, resealable plastic bag and freeze it until solid.

Pry the mixture out of the bag and place it in a fine mesh strainer set over a mixing bowl. Allow it to thaw completely so the clear liquid drains into the bowl.

Transfer the tomato residue to a wet linen tea towel and squeeze it gently to extract as much clear liquid as possible. Stir in the celery bitters and fish sauce, and refrigerate until ready to use.

Rim 6 stemmed martini glasses with celery salt, if desired, following the instructions on page 56–57.

Pour 2 tablespoons of the tomato water and 1½ to 2 ounces of the vodka into a cocktail shaker filled with ice cubes. Stir it well.

Strain the drink into a rimmed glass using a funnel to avoid wetting the rim. Garnish each drink with a toothpick of cherry tomatoes and rest a shrimp on the rim of the glass. Serve immediately.

Note: The mix can be made up to 2 days in advance and refrigerated, tightly covered.

stemmed martini

ORZO ARANCINI ALLA MILANESE

I developed a version of this easy snack for my book *Mac & Cheese: 80 Classic & Creative Versions of the Ultimate Comfort Food* and now I really prefer them to the traditional balls made from leftover risotto. The crispy yet creamy balls are a perfect foil to a spicy Bloody Mary.

Makes 3 dozen

½ pound orzo
⅔ cup chicken stock
Pinch of saffron
¼ cup (½ stick) unsalted butter
1 large shallot, chopped
1 cup all-purpose flour, divided
½ cup heavy cream, heated
¼ cup dry white wine
1 tablespoon chopped fresh parsley
1 teaspoon fresh thyme leaves
⅔ cup freshly grated Parmesan cheese
Salt and freshly ground black pepper
4 large eggs, well beaten, divided
2 tablespoons whole milk
2 cups panko breadcrumbs
Vegetable oil for frying
Marinara sauce for serving (optional)

Bring a pot of salted water to a boil over high heat. Cook the pasta until it is past al dente and is soft. Drain the pasta and return it to the pot.

Place the chicken stock in a small saucepan, crumble in the saffron, and bring to a boil over high heat. Cook until only ¼ cup remains. Set aside.

Heat the butter in a saucepan over medium-low heat. Add the shallot and cook for 3 minutes, or until the shallot is translucent. Stir in 3 tablespoons of the flour and cook, stirring constantly, for 1 minute, or until the mixture turns slightly beige, is bubbly, and appears to have grown in volume. Increase the heat to medium, and slowly whisk in the reduced stock, cream, and wine. Bring to a boil, whisking frequently. Reduce the heat to low, stir in the parsley and thyme, and simmer the sauce for 2 minutes. Add the cheese to the sauce ¼ cup at a time, stirring until the cheese melts before making another addition. Pour the sauce over the pasta, and stir well. Season with salt and pepper to taste. Place the pasta in a mixing bowl and chill well.

Stir one quarter of the beaten eggs into the pasta mixture. Form balls using 1½-tablespoon portions of the pasta mixture and place them on a sheet of plastic wrap.

Place the remaining flour in a shallow bowl. Combine the remaining eggs with the milk in another shallow bowl, and whisk well. Place the breadcrumbs in a third bowl.

Coat the balls with the flour, shaking to remove any excess. Dip the balls in the egg wash, and then immediately into the bread-crumbs. Pat the balls gently so that the crumbs adhere. Line a baking sheet with plastic wrap and return the balls to the refrigerator for at least 30 minutes, or until ready to cook.

To serve, heat 2 inches of oil in a deep-sided skillet or Dutch oven over high heat to 350°F. Fry the pasta balls in the hot oil. Be careful to not crowd the pan. Cook for 2 to 3 minutes, turning them gently with a slotted spoon, or until browned. Drain well on paper towels, and serve immediately with marinara sauce for dipping, if desired.

Note: The balls can be fried up to 2 days in advance and refrigerated, tightly covered. Reheat them in a 375°F oven for 4 to 6 minutes, or until hot.

Variations: Press ½-inch cubes of mozzarella, Gruyère, Swiss, or Cheddar cheese in the center of each ball. Add 3 ounces chopped prosciutto or salami to the pasta.

Sunrise Surprise

This drink fools some people when it's placed in front of them; they assume it's going to be sweet and fruity because the color is that of orange juice. But yellow tomatoes, some of the sweetest that can be grown, form the basis for this refreshing and somewhat spicy summer sipper.

Makes 6 drinks

3 pounds yellow tomatoes, cored and diced

1 tablespoon kosher salt

¾ cup dill pickle brine

¼ cup freshly squeezed lime juice

3 tablespoons Mexican hot sauce, such as Cholula, or more to taste

3 tablespoons Tajín for rimming the glasses (optional)

9 to 12 ounces vodka or Bacon-Infused Vodka (page 41)

SUGGESTED GARNISHES:

Spears of dill pickle

Skewers of multicolored cherry tomatoes

Skewers of jalapeño Jack or Manchego cheese

Strips of Beef Jerky (page 153) or store-bought jerky

Combine the tomatoes and salt in a food processor, and purée until smooth. Transfer the mixture to a container and refrigerate for 2 to 4 hours to allow the foam to subside. Strain the mixture through a sieve, pressing with the back of a spoon to extract as much liquid as possible.

Combine the tomato juice, brine, lime juice, and hot sauce in a pitcher and stir well. Chill well.

Rim 6 (14-ounce) glasses with Tajín, if desired, following the instructions on page 56–57.

Pour about 6 ounces (¾ cup) of the mix into a pint glass, add 1½ to 2 ounces of the vodka, and fill the glass completely with ice. Roll the drink between 2 pint glasses to mix and chill for individual servings (see page 59), or pour the vodka and mix into a pitcher filled with ice and stir well with a long-handled spoon.

Strain the drink into a rimmed glass using a funnel to avoid wetting the rim. Add ice cubes, and garnish each drink with a spear of dill pickle, skewers of cherry tomatoes and cheese cubes, and a strip of jerky. Serve immediately.

Note: The mix can be made up to 2 days in advance and refrigerated, tightly covered.

double old-fashioned

SPICED MIXED NUTS

A bowl of aromatic and vibrantly flavored mixed nuts is always a hit with guests, and this combination, with both dried and fresh herbs and spices, goes especially well with Bloody Marys. Egg white is like a natural glue for foods, be it holding herbs on these nuts or caraway seeds on the crust of a rye bread.

Makes 3 cups

3 cups raw, unsalted mixed nuts (some combination of peanuts, almonds, cashews, pecans, and filberts)
1 large egg white, at room temperature
1 teaspoon kosher salt
¼ cup granulated sugar
1 tablespoon Tajín or Old Bay seasoning
1 tablespoon chopped fresh rosemary leaves
1 teaspoon chopped fresh thyme leaves
¼ teaspoon cayenne pepper
2 tablespoons unsalted butter, melted and cooled
3 tablespoons freshly grated Parmesan cheese

Preheat the oven to 300°F and line a baking sheet with parchment paper or a silicone baking mat.

Arrange the nuts on the baking sheet and toast them for 20 minutes, stirring them after 10 minutes. Allow the nuts to cool for 10 minutes.

Whisk the egg white and salt until frothy in a mixing bowl. Add the sugar, 1 tablespoon at a time, and continue to whisk until soft peaks form. Beat in the Tajín, rosemary, thyme, and cayenne. Add the cooled nuts, butter, and cheese, and coat them evenly with the egg mixture.

Spread the nuts in a single layer on the baking sheet and bake them for 25 to 30 minutes, or until they are golden brown. Cool the nuts for at least 15 minutes before serving.

Note: The nuts can be stored in an airtight container at room temperature for up to 1 week.

Spiced Mixed Nuts and Deviled Eggs Niçoise (page 116)

DEVILED EGGS NIÇOISE

There's a special place in my heart for deviled eggs. Everyone loves them: Just look at how fast they're eaten at summer parties. Salade niçoise always includes hard-cooked eggs, so for this flavorful deviled egg riff the other ingredients in the famed salad are included in the yolk filling.

Makes 1 dozen

6 hard-cooked eggs, peeled and halved lengthwise
9 red cherry or grape tomatoes, divided
½ cup light tuna packed in oil, drained
2 tablespoons chopped oil-cured black olives
2 tablespoons bottled Italian dressing
2 tablespoons mayonnaise
2 teaspoons freshly squeezed lemon juice
1 teaspoon Dijon mustard
Salt and freshly ground black pepper
3 fresh basil leaves, thinly sliced

Cut the eggs in half lengthwise, remove the yolks from the whites, and grate the yolks through the large holes on a box grater into a mixing bowl. Chop 6 of the tomatoes and shake them in a sieve.

Add the chopped tomatoes, tuna, olives, Italian dressing, mayonnaise, lemon juice, and mustard to the bowl with the egg yolks. Stir with a rubber spatula to combine the mixture, and then season with salt and pepper to taste.

Slice the remaining cherry tomatoes into quarters lengthwise. Mound the yolk mixture into the egg whites, and top each with a slice of tomato and a few basil shreds. Serve immediately.

Note: The yolk mixture can be prepared 1 day in advance and refrigerated, tightly covered.

Hard-Cooked Eggs Explained

The trickiest part of making deviled eggs is boiling the eggs so that they peel easily without the white bonding with the shell, and here's my foolproof method. Bring a large saucepan of water to a boil over high heat. It should be large enough that the eggs can cook in one layer, and you want enough water in the pan so that it returns quickly to a boil. Add cold eggs right out of the refrigerator, cover the pan, and bring the water back to a boil. Reduce the heat to low and simmer the eggs, uncovered, for eleven minutes. Use a timer so you don't overcook them. Plunge the hot eggs into a large mixing bowl of ice water, and let them cool until chilled in the water. Crack the shells all over against the sides of the mixing bowl, and then begin to peel them starting with the large end.

Using this method you'll find that the white remains tender instead of becoming rubbery and there's no ugly green ring around the yolk. The gross color is iron sulfide, and it happens when the iron in the egg yolk reacts to the hydrogen sulfide in the egg white when an egg is woefully overcooked. Unlike when other foods are overcooked, however, the eggs are totally edible, even though they're tough and dry.

Bullshots are a Blast from the Past

From the mid 1950s to the start of the Reagan administration the Bullshot was everywhere. Gossip columnist Dorothy Kilgallen heralded its popularity with everyone from fashion models to movie producers on the West Coast, and it was *the* drink to order for those inhabitants of the tony Upper East Side of New York City whose names always appeared in boldface. By the end of the 1970s people were becoming more interested in gyms than supper clubs, and the white wine spritzer elbowed out the Bullshot along with spirits like bourbon and Scotch. But now it's back on the lists of restaurants such as Gabrielle Hamilton's Prune in New York City.

Bullshot

Now that bone broths are all the rage, there's been a renaissance of popularity for a drink from the mid twentieth century that swapped out the tomato juice in a Bloody Mary with strong beef consommé, the Bullshot. Celery bitters give it a modern twist, but this recipe is fairly true to its original form.

Makes 6 drinks

2 cups double-strength beef consommé, such as Campbell's

2 tablespoons freshly squeezed lemon juice

1 tablespoon Worcestershire sauce

1 tablespoon celery bitters

1 to 2 teaspoons hot red pepper sauce, or more to taste

3 tablespoons celery salt for rimming the glasses (optional)

9 to 12 ounces vodka or Bacon-Infused Vodka (page 41)

SUGGESTED GARNISHES:

Strips of Beef Jerky (page 153) or store-bought jerky

Lemon wedges

Celery sticks with leaves

Toothpick with green olives alternated with cherry tomatoes

Coarsely ground black pepper

Combine the consommé, lemon juice, Worcestershire sauce, celery bitters, and hot red pepper sauce in a pitcher and stir well.

Rim 6 (10-ounce) glasses with celery salt, if desired, following the instructions on page 56–57.

For each drink, pour 4 ounces (½ cup) of the mix and 1½ to 2 ounces of the vodka into a cocktail shaker filled with ice cubes. Shake well. Strain into a rimmed glass using a funnel to avoid wetting the rim. Add ice cubes, and garnish each drink with beef jerky, a lemon wedge, a celery stick, and a toothpick of olives and cherry tomatoes. Coarsely grind some black pepper over the surface. Serve immediately.

Note: The mix can be made up to 2 days in advance and refrigerated, tightly covered.

Variation: For a Warm Bullshot, dilute the mix with 1½ cups water and heat it in a small saucepan over medium heat until warm. Then divide the mix into glass mugs, add the vodka, and garnish the mug.

old-fashioned

Hold the Tomatoes Martini

If you love everything about a Bloody Mary except for the tomato part, here's a rather potent drink that should be perfect for you. Your choice of vodka or gin is infused with all the powerful flavoring ingredients that add zing to a good mix, sans the tomato juice. It's then served straight up, the way any good martini should be. Please note that this is not an impromptu drink because the mixture needs two days to infuse.

Makes 6 drinks

16 ounces (2 cups) vodka or gin
¼ cup diced fresh horseradish (no need to peel)
1 celery rib, diced
1 jalapeño or serrano chile, stemmed and sliced (leave the seeds in)
1 tablespoon cracked black peppercorns
Grated zest of 2 lemons
1 garlic clove, minced (optional)
¼ cup freshly squeezed lemon juice
2 tablespoons green olive brine
2 tablespoons Thai fish sauce (nam pla)
3 tablespoons celery salt for rimming the glasses (optional)

SUGGESTED GARNISHES:
Toothpicks with a green olive, cornichon, and cocktail onion
Sun-dried tomato halves (dry packed; not in olive oil) cut halfway up to form a slit

stemmed martini

Combine the liquor, horseradish, celery, chile, peppercorns, lemon zest, and garlic, if using, in a glass jar and shake well. Add the lemon juice, brine, and fish sauce and shake well again. Allow the mixture to sit on the counter for 2 days, shaking it occasionally.

Line a fine-mesh strainer with a double layer of cheesecloth or strong paper towels and pour the liquid through it into a mixing bowl. Press with the back of a spoon to extract as much liquid as possible. Transfer the liquor to a glass jar and refrigerate.

Rim 6 stemmed martini glasses with celery salt, if desired, following the instructions on page 56–57.

For each drink, pour about 3½ ounces of the liquor in a shaker filled with ice cubes. Stir well. Strain into a rimmed glass using a funnel to avoid wetting the rim. Garnish each drink with a toothpick with an olive, a cornichon, and a cocktail onion, and balance a sun-dried tomato half on the rim of the glass. Serve immediately.

Note: The liquor can be refrigerated for up to 3 months. It can also be frozen for up to 6 months, but the lemon juice and olive brine will freeze. Allow it to sit out at room temperature until it becomes clear.

Michelada

It's not just Americans who sometimes crave "the hair of the dog," but in Mexico, where the Michelada is the traditional drink for the problem of a hangover, it may be called *el pelo del perro*. The Michelada, pronounced *mee-chay-LAH-dah*, is beer spiked with tomato juice, lime juice, and hot sauce. While the lime wedges are traditional, I also like to garnish this drink with some cheese and beef for protein and some vegetables, too.

Makes 6 drinks

⅔ cup tomato juice
¼ cup freshly squeezed lime juice
2 to 3 tablespoons Mexican hot sauce, such as
    Cholula, or more to taste
3 (12-ounce) cans or bottles of pale Mexican beer

GLASS RIM (OPTIONAL):
2 tablespoons kosher salt
1 tablespoon chili powder

SUGGESTED GARNISHES:
Lime wedges
Skewers of multicolored cherry tomatoes and
    green olives
Skewers of cubed jalapeño Jack cheese
Strips of Beef Jerky (page 153) or store-bought
    jerky

Combine the tomato juice, lime juice, and hot sauce in a pitcher, and stir well. Chill until ready to serve.

Rim 6 (16-ounce) glasses with a combination of salt and chili powder, if desired, following the instructions on page 56–57.

Add about 3 ounces of the tomato mixture to each rimmed glass using a funnel to avoid wetting the rim. Add ice cubes, and then slowly pour 6 ounces of beer into each glass. Garnish each drink with a lime wedge, a skewer of tomatoes and olives, a skewer of cheese cubes, and a few slices of jerky. Serve immediately.

Note: The mix can be made up to 2 days in advance and refrigerated, tightly covered.

pilsner

MUFFULETTA QUESADILLA

There are many versions of an overstuffed Italian sandwich that were invented in the twentieth century as a way for delis to use up the ends of cold cuts and cheeses. The muffuletta, made on a round loaf of bread and topped with olive salad, hails from Central Grocery in the French Quarter of New Orleans.

Makes 2 dozen pieces

Vegetable oil spray
1 cup pimiento-stuffed green olives
3 garlic cloves, minced
2 tablespoons chopped fresh parsley
1 tablespoon olive oil
1 tablespoon white wine vinegar
6 (8-inch) flour tortillas
6 slices mortadella (about 4 ounces)
6 slices baked ham (about 4 ounces)
12 slices Genoa salami (about 4 ounces)
6 slices provolone cheese (about 4 ounces)

Note: The quesadillas can be assembled 1 day before cooking. Refrigerate them separated by layers of plastic wrap.

Preheat the oven to 450°F. Cover a baking sheet with heavy-duty aluminum foil and coat the foil with vegetable oil spray.

In a food processor, chop the olives finely, using on-and-off pulsing. Transfer the olives to a small mixing bowl and add the garlic, parsley, olive oil, and vinegar. Stir well and set aside.

Wrap the tortillas in plastic wrap and microwave on high for 20 to 30 seconds, or until they are warm and pliable. Place the tortillas so that one half of each circle is on the baking sheet. Layer the mortadella, ham, salami, and cheese on the half of each tortilla resting on the baking sheet. Sprinkle 1 heaping tablespoon of the olive topping over the filling. Fold the blank side of the tortillas over the filling and press them closed with the palm of your hand or a spatula.

Arrange the quesadillas so they are evenly spaced on the baking sheet. Spray the tops of the tortillas with vegetable oil spray.

Bake the quesadillas in the center of the oven for 5 minutes. Turn them with a spatula, Return them to the oven for 5 minutes, or until browned. Allow them to sit for 3 minutes, then cut each into 4 wedges and serve.

BLACK BEAN SPREAD

This easy vegetarian spread has all the tantalizing flavors of traditional Southwestern food, and it's a snap to make since it uses canned beans. Serve it with tortilla chips or crudité for scooping.

Makes 4 cups

⅓ cup olive oil
1 small red onion, chopped
3 garlic cloves, minced
2 (15-ounce) cans black beans, drained and rinsed
½ cup sour cream
¼ cup freshly squeezed lime juice
1 tablespoon chopped fresh oregano leaves
2 teaspoons ground coriander
2 teaspoons ground cumin
1 teaspoon hot red pepper sauce, or more to taste
½ cup chopped pimientos
¼ cup chopped fresh cilantro
Salt

Heat the oil in a skillet over medium heat. Add the onion and garlic and cook, stirring frequently, for 3 minutes, or until the onion is translucent. Scrape the mixture into a mixing bowl and set aside.

Combine the beans, sour cream, lime juice, oregano, coriander, cumin, and hot red pepper sauce in a food processor, and purée until smooth. Scrape the mixture into the mixing bowl with the vegetables. Stir in the pimientos and cilantro and season with salt to taste. Refrigerate until well chilled.

Note: The spread can be made 4 days in advance and refrigerated, tightly covered.

Blushing Pink Adobe

In many regions Mexican cuisine includes dishes that combine vegetables and fruits and achieve an almost sweet-and-sour profile. That's what you'll find when sipping this refreshing libation. And using a flavorful liquor just adds to its complexity. This is great with the varied fare found in Latin America.

Makes 6 drinks

3 cups diced seedless watermelon

1 cup strained tomatoes (passata di pomodoro)

1 cup diced peeled cucumber

1 to 2 chipotle chiles in adobo sauce

2 to 3 tablespoons adobo sauce, or more to taste

⅓ cup freshly squeezed lime juice

2 tablespoons agave nectar

1 tablespoon orange bitters

¼ cup chopped fresh cilantro

Smoked salt

3 tablespoons Tajín for rimming the glasses (optional)

9 to 12 ounces tequila, pisco, or cachaça

SUGGESTED GARNISHES:

Lime wedges

Skewers of watermelon cubes

Skewers of Ceviche (page 161)

Sprigs of fresh cilantro

Place the watermelon, strained tomatoes, cucumber, chiles, and adobo sauce in a food processor or blender, and purée until smooth. Strain the liquid through a sieve, pressing with the back of a spoon to extract as much liquid as possible.

Combine the strained liquid with the lime juice, agave nectar, orange bitters, and chopped cilantro in a pitcher, and stir well. Season with smoked salt to taste, and chill well.

Rim 6 (14-ounce) glasses with Tajín, if desired, following the instructions on page 56–57.

Pour about 6 ounces (¾ cup) of the mix into a pint glass, add 1½ to 2 ounces of liquor, and fill the glass completely with ice. Roll the drink between 2 pint glasses to mix and chill for individual servings (see page 59), or pour the liquor and mix into a pitcher filled with ice and stir well with a long-handled spoon.

Strain the drink into a rimmed glass using a funnel to avoid wetting the rim. Add ice cubes, and garnish each drink with a lime wedge, a skewer of watermelon cubes, a skewer of ceviche, and sprigs of cilantro. Serve immediately.

Note: The mix can be made up to 2 days in advance and refrigerated, tightly covered.

highball

Avocado Cooler

Creamy avocados create a totally luxurious mouth-feel in this drink that has some spiciness from both fresh chiles and wasabi powder, along with some sweetness from puréed green grapes.

Makes 6 drinks

½ English cucumber, diced
½ pound tomatillos, husked, rinsed, cored, and diced
1½ ripe avocados, peeled and diced
1½ cups green seedless grapes
½ cup firmly packed fresh cilantro leaves
1 large jalapeño or serrano chile, seeds and ribs removed
⅓ cup freshly squeezed lime juice
1 tablespoon orange bitters
1 to 2 teaspoons wasabi powder, or more to taste
Salt and freshly ground black pepper
3 tablespoons Tajín for rimming the glasses (optional)
9 to 12 ounces vodka or Spicy Vodka (page 43)

SUGGESTED GARNISHES:
Avocado slices
Skewers of red cherry tomatoes
Skewers of Ceviche (page 161)
Strips of orange bell pepper

Place the cucumber, tomatillos, avocados, grapes, cilantro, and chile in a food processor or blender, and purée until smooth. Strain the liquid through a sieve, pressing with the back of a spoon to extract as much liquid as possible.

Combine the strained purée with the lime juice, bitters, and wasabi in a pitcher. Add enough water to equal 4½ cups, and stir well. Season with salt and pepper to taste, and chill.

Rim 6 (14-ounce) glasses with Tajín, if desired, following the instructions on page 56–57.

Pour about 6 ounces (¾ cup) of the mix into a pint glass, add 1½ to 2 ounces of the vodka, and fill the glass completely with ice. Roll the drink between 2 pint glasses to mix and chill for individual servings (see page 59), or pour the vodka and mix into a pitcher filled with ice and stir well with a long-handled spoon.

Strain the drink into a rimmed glass using a funnel to avoid wetting the rim. Add ice cubes, and garnish the drink with an avocado slice, a skewer of cherry tomatoes, a skewer of ceviche, and strips of bell pepper. Serve immediately.

Note: The mix can be made up to 2 hours in advance and refrigerated. Press a sheet of plastic wrap directly into the surface to prevent discoloration.

highball

CRISPY SPICED GARBANZO BEANS

Perhaps because of their meaty texture, or maybe it's due to their nut-like flavor, but I think that garbanzo beans are one of the most satisfying legumes to eat. Once you taste them crispy and fried you'll be adding this addictive snack to your repertoire.

Makes 3 cups

2 (15-ounce) cans garbanzo beans, drained and rinsed
1 tablespoon ground coriander
1 tablespoon ground cumin
1 tablespoon chili powder
½ cup all-purpose flour
Vegetable oil for frying
Kosher salt and freshly ground black pepper

Line a baking sheet with paper towels and spread the beans on the paper. Blot the tops of the beans with additional towels. Transfer the beans to a mixing bowl.

Combine the coriander, cumin, and chili powder in a small bowl, and toss the mixture with the beans. Sprinkle the flour over the beans and toss to coat them well. Place the beans in a sieve and shake it over the sink or a garbage can to get rid of extra flour.

Heat 2 inches of oil in a deep-sided saucepan to 350°F. Add half of the beans and fry them for about 6 minutes, or until they are browned and crisp. Remove the beans from the oil with a slotted spoon and drain them well on paper towels. Fry the remaining beans in the same fashion.

Sprinkle the beans liberally with salt and pepper to taste, and serve.

Note: The beans can be fried up to 2 hours in advance and kept at room temperature.

Variation: Substitute Italian seasoning or herbes de Provence for the coriander, cumin, and chili powder.

Tomatillo Treat

Tart and tangy tomatillos, which make for a great drink, have gotten increasingly easy to find even in parts of the country that don't boast a significant Hispanic population. I'm especially fond of preparing this recipe with Chilean or Peruvian pisco, but Mexican tequila or Brazilian cachaça are equally good. Try this drink with huevos rancheros or a breakfast burrito.

Makes 6 drinks

1 pound tomatillos, husked, rinsed, cored, and diced
½ English cucumber, diced
2 jalapeño or serrano chiles, seeds and ribs removed
2 large garlic cloves
½ cup firmly packed cilantro leaves
⅓ cup freshly squeezed lime juice
1 tablespoon granulated sugar
Salt and freshly ground white pepper
3 tablespoons Tajín for rimming the glasses (optional)
9 to 12 ounces tequila, pisco, or cachaça

SUGGESTED GARNISHES:
Avocado wedges
Lime wedges
Skewers of Ceviche (page 161) or boiled shrimp
Skewers of cherry tomatoes

Place the tomatillos, cucumber, chiles, garlic, cilantro, lime juice, and sugar in a food processor or blender, and purée until smooth. Strain the liquid through a sieve, pressing with the back of a spoon to extract as much liquid as possible. Add cold water, if necessary, to make 4½ cups of mix. Chill well.

Rim 6 (14-ounce) glasses with Tajín, if desired, following the instructions on page 56–57.

Pour about 6 ounces (¾ cup) of the mix into a pint glass, add 1½ to 2 ounces of liquor, and fill the glass completely with ice. Roll the drink between 2 pint glasses to mix and chill for individual servings (see page 59), or pour the liquor and mix into a pitcher filled with ice and stir well with a long-handled spoon.

Strain the drink into a rimmed glass using a funnel to avoid wetting the rim. Add ice cubes, and garnish each drink with avocado and lime wedges, a skewer of ceviche, and a skewer of cherry tomatoes. Serve immediately.

Note: The mix can be made up to 2 days in advance and refrigerated, tightly covered.

snifter

THAT CILANTRO FLAVOR

Few foods are as polarizing as cilantro. People either love it or hate it. Julia Child was in the latter camp and agreed with those who thought that cilantro smelled like soap and tasted like crushed beetles. There's even a website, ihatecilantro. com, where people with this pathological aversion to this herb with lacy green leaves can purchase T-shirts to let others know. But scientists have now concluded that a dislike of cilantro is hardwired into our DNA. There are four genes related to sensory perception that are different in people who love or abhor cilantro. Always remember, flat-leaf parsley is a great substitute.

Tomatillo Treats with Ceviche (page 161)

SOUTHWEST SMOKED SALMON PINWHEELS

There are a number of drinks in this book that have Mexican overtones, either from the use of tequila or from the inclusion of ingredients such as tomatillos and chipotle chiles in the Bloody Mary mix. These easy-to-make wraps slice into gorgeous pinwheels with bright salmon surrounding a center of mixed greens, the colors of the Mexican flag. You can also thread them onto a skewer and use them as a garnish.

Makes 2 dozen pieces

1 cup good-quality refrigerated tomato salsa (do not use bottled salsa)
4 ounces cream cheese, at room temperature
¼ cup chopped fresh cilantro
4 (8-inch) flour tortillas
½ pound thinly sliced smoked salmon
2 cups mesclun salad mix or other baby greens

Drain the salsa in a strainer, pressing with the back of a spoon to extract as much liquid as possible. Combine the drained salsa, cream cheese, and cilantro in a mixing bowl and stir well.

Wrap the tortillas in plastic wrap and microwave for 20 to 30 seconds, or until soft and pliable.

Place the tortillas on a counter, and spread each with the cream cheese mixture. Arrange the salmon slices on the bottom half of each tortilla. Place ½ cup of the mesclun at the bottom edge of the tortilla on top of the salmon. Roll the tortillas firmly but gently starting at the filled edge. Place the rolls, seam-side down, on a platter or ungreased baking sheet, and refrigerate for 1 hour.

Trim the end of each roll by cutting on the diagonal to remove the portion of the tortilla that does not meet and form a log. Cut each tortilla into 6 slices and serve chilled.

Note: The tortillas can be filled up to 6 hours in advance and refrigerated, tightly covered with plastic wrap. Slice them just before serving.

Variation: Substitute thinly sliced smoked turkey or smoked ham for the smoked salmon.

Mixed Sangrita

Sangrita hails from the Jalisco region of Mexico, home to Cholula Hot Sauce, Tajín seasoning and—most importantly—tequila. In its native land this blending of juices and spices is a chaser to a shot of straight tequila. But it's also delicious spiked with the agave spirit, and for variety you might also like it with other Latin American liquors such as pisco or cachaça.

Makes 6 drinks

2 cups tomato juice
¾ cup freshly squeezed orange juice
½ cup pomegranate juice
½ cup strained tomatoes (passata di pomodoro)
¼ cup freshly squeezed lime juice
2 tablespoons Mexican hot sauce, such as Cholula,
   or more to taste
3 tablespoons Tajín for rimming the glasses
   (optional)
9 to 12 ounces tequila

SUGGESTED GARNISHES:
Orange slices
Pomegranate seeds
Skewers of Ceviche (page 161)
Skewers of cubed jalapeño Jack or Manchego
   cheese

Combine the tomato juice, orange juice, pomegranate juice, strained tomatoes, lime juice, and hot sauce in a pitcher, and stir well. Chill well.

Rim 6 (14-ounce) glasses with Tajín, if desired, following the instructions on page 56–57.

Pour about 6 ounces (¾ cup) of the mix into a pint glass, add 1½ to 2 ounces of the tequila, and fill the glass completely with ice. Roll the drink between 2 pint glasses to mix and chill for individual servings (see page 59), or pour the tequila and mix into a pitcher filled with ice and stir well with a long-handled spoon.

Strain the drink into a rimmed glass using a funnel to avoid wetting the rim. Add ice cubes, and garnish each drink with an orange slice on the rim, a sprinkling of pomegranate seeds, a skewer of ceviche, and a skewer of cheese. Serve immediately.

Note: The mix can be made up to 2 days in advance and refrigerated, tightly covered.

collins

CHILEAN POTATO PUFFS (PAPAS DUQUESAS)

These crispy puffs are like little pillows of flavor, and they're a perfect snack to serve with any and all drinks. They can also be made in advance and reheated, which makes them a great party dish.

Makes 3 dozen pieces

2½ pounds russet potatoes, peeled and
    cut into 2-inch chunks
¼ cup (½ stick) unsalted butter
1 shallot, chopped
2 garlic cloves, minced
3 large eggs, beaten, divided
½ cup all-purpose flour, plus more for dredging
⅓ cup freshly grated Parmesan cheese
2 tablespoons chopped fresh parsley
Salt and freshly ground black pepper
½ cup whole milk
2 cups plain dry breadcrumbs
Vegetable oil for frying

Notes: The puffs can be made up to 2 days in advance and refrigerated in a single layer, tightly covered with plastic wrap. Reheat them in a 375°F oven for 3 to 5 minutes, or until hot and crisp.

    The reason to chill food prior to frying is to allow the layers of coating to bond together. The flour, eggs, and breadcrumbs become much stronger once chilled.

Boil the potatoes in salted water to cover for 15 to 20 minutes, or until they are very tender. Drain the potatoes. Push them through a potato ricer or food mill, and place them in a mixing bowl.

While the potatoes boil, melt the butter in a small skillet over medium heat. Add the shallot and garlic and cook, stirring frequently, for 5 to 7 minutes, or until the shallot is tender. Add the shallot mixture, one third of the beaten eggs, and the flour, cheese, and parsley to the potatoes. Season with salt and pepper to taste, and mix well.

Form the mixture into 1-inch balls. Place some flour in a shallow bowl, combine the remaining eggs with the milk in another shallow bowl, and place the breadcrumbs in a third shallow bowl. Dredge the balls in the flour, dip them in the egg, and then roll them in the breadcrumbs, pressing gently to get the coating to adhere. Chill the balls on a baking sheet lined with plastic wrap for at least 30 minutes, or up to 1 day.

Preheat the oven to 175°F, and place a few layers of paper towels on a baking sheet. Heat 2 inches of oil in a deep-sided saucepan to 350°F.

Fry the puffs, being careful not to crowd the pan, for 2½ to 3 minutes, or until evenly brown and crisp. Remove the puffs from the oil with a slotted spoon and drain on paper towels. Keep the puffs warm in the oven while frying the remainder. Serve immediately.

Variations: Add ½ cup fried and crumbled bacon or sausage, substitute Cheddar or Swiss cheese for the Parmesan, or substitute Cajun seasoning for the salt and pepper.

Tropical Tango

Whereas tequila has been popular north of the border for decades, such interesting liquors such as cachaça from Brazil and pisco from Chile and Peru are just coming into the spotlight. Their flavor is wonderful with this combination of sweet and tart fruit flavors balanced by spices.

Makes 6 drinks

1 juicing orange

2 ripe yellow Champagne (Ataulfo) mangoes, peeled and diced

5 scallions, white parts only, sliced

1 ¼ cups freshly squeezed grapefruit juice

⅔ cup unseasoned rice vinegar

2 jalapeño or serrano chiles, seeds and ribs removed, diced

3 garlic cloves

3 tablespoons diced fresh ginger

½ orange bell pepper, seeds and ribs removed, diced

½ English cucumber, peeled and diced

Salt

Mexican hot sauce, such as Cholula

9 to 12 ounces tequila, pisco, cachaça, or light rum

GLASS RIM (OPTIONAL):

1½ tablespoons kosher salt

1½ tablespoons chili powder

SUGGESTED GARNISHES:

Strips of orange or red bell pepper

Sprigs of fresh cilantro

Skewers of Ceviche (page 161) or boiled shrimp

Skewers of cubed mango

Lime wedges

highball

Grate the zest from the orange and squeeze out the orange juice. Combine the orange zest, orange juice, mangoes, scallions, grapefruit juice, vinegar, chiles, garlic, ginger, bell pepper, and cucumber in a food processor or blender. Purée until smooth.

Strain half of the mixture through a fine sieve, pressing with the back of a spoon to extract as much liquid as possible. Stir the liquid into the unstrained portion, and season with salt and hot sauce to taste. Chill well.

Rim 6 (14-ounce) glasses with a combination of salt and chili powder, if desired, following the instructions on page 56–57.

Pour about 6 ounces (¾ cup) of the mix into a pint glass, add 1½ to 2 ounces of the liquor, and fill the glass completely with ice. Roll the drink between 2 pint glasses to mix and chill for individual servings (see page 59), or pour the liquor and mix into a pitcher filled with ice and stir well with a long-handled spoon.

Strain the drink into a rimmed glass using a funnel to avoid wetting the rim. Add ice cubes, and garnish each drink with strips of bell pepper, sprigs of cilantro, a skewer of ceviche, a skewer of mango, and a lime wedge. Serve immediately.

Note: The mix can be made up to 2 days in advance and refrigerated, tightly covered.

There's an easy way to cut decorative cubes out of a mango. The pit is elliptical and runs the length of the fruit. Slice off both sides of the flesh around the pit without peeling the mango, then score the flesh in a diamond pattern and turn the skin inside out. The flesh will pop away from the peel, making it easy to cut the cubes off.

CHAPTER 5

It's All About the Garnishes

At Sobelman's Pub & Grill in Milwaukee there's a fried chicken—I mean the *whole bird*—propped up on the rim of a 60-ounce Bloody Mary. And that's just one of the garnishes; there are skewers of bacon-wrapped jalapeño cheese cubes, Brussels sprouts, shrimp, asparagus spears, and sausages. There are restaurants perching grilled ribs across the rims of glasses, using strips of beef jerky as swizzle sticks, and indulging many aquatic fantasies.

What tops the drinks has become as important as the contents of the glass to many people, and when Bloody Marys are served at a restaurant with a full kitchen rather than at a bar with a cubbyhole for lemon wedges, many cooks get very creative. While an endless pitcher of Bloody Marys might be an inducement for brunch, other restaurants are putting so much on top of the glass that it *becomes* brunch. It's smart marketing; they can charge a premium for the drink and the person sits on a barstool rather than claiming prime real estate at a table.

The great thing about building this kind of Temple of Temptation is that you can buy all the foods. You really don't have to make a single, solitary thing.

This chapter is divided into categories of garnishes. Think of it as the old Chinese restaurant menu; pick one from column A and two from column B. Or in this case, choose a meat, a seafood, and a few types of something vegetal. There remains a place for the celery rib, even in this world of shrimp and sliders.

But there may be times that you want to prepare a signature garnish that your guests would not have nibbled the night before, so there are some recipes in this chapter for those.

Selecting Foods to Stack

Though there are literally thousands of foods from which to choose, the litmus test remains the same: Will it add to the pleasure of the drink? That's why the vast majority of foods on these lists are savory, salty, sour, and spicy. They tie to the basic flavor profile of a traditional Bloody Mary. While maple-glazed bacon might be an option, the sweetness is a balance to the basic saltiness of the bacon.

Flavor compatibility is the goal. If the drink has Italian overtones, such as the Sicilian Sipper (page 89), then a skewer of grilled Italian sausage would be a better choice than a skewer of bratwurst or kielbasa. But these other porcine pleasures harmonize nicely with the flavors in the Ballpark Bloody (page 75).

Then unless you're going for a dramatic monochromatic look—all green garnishes, for example—you want your garnish portfolio to have a lot of color variation, even if there isn't that much textural variation. For an easy solution there's no better friend than the panoply of peppers in the produce department; it's a color riot of red, yellow, orange, and purple.

In restaurants the up-and-coming trend is to include hot items on the "totem of treats," but I don't really endorse that when you're serving at home because doing so requires last-minute reheating, if not cooking, which also means that the drinks can't be prepared in advance.

Building Your Structure

If you have a degree in mechanical engineering you're at a distinct advantage when it comes to creating the framework for an awe-inspiring Bloody Mary garnish. But even we mere mortals can make it stunning with some imagination and some strong skewers.

All skewers are not created equal. The thin ones commonly found in supermarkets for dishes like chicken satay are good for light-weight, fairly soft foods. For heftier and harder foods, you need to find nice thick bamboo skewers, or get some reusable metal ones.

When you look at a glass there are three possible ways that food can be arranged: vertically, horizontally, and perched on the rim. The verticals are easy; just make sure that your skewers are long enough to reach the bottom of the glass. That will stabilize the skewer and all the foods on it. You also have to measure to make sure that you've left enough of the skewer bare that your foods won't end up in the soup, or in this case, in the Bloody Mary. Always work your way up from the largest item to the small-est item on the skewer, so a whole pepperoncini would go on first and a small rosette of smoked salmon would be at the tip.

But vertical skewers are not really vertical, they're askew unless you anchor them to a horizontal for increased stability. That's where your friend the celery rib or carrot stick comes to the rescue. Before starting to thread your foods, begin by drilling through the middle of the celery or carrot, which will rest on the rim of the glass horizontally and keep everything straight. You can stick a celery rib with two or three skewers of garnish, too.

For the horizontal elements you should use shorter skewers and toothpicks and anchor them to the sides of the celery. You can also just drape items like crisp slices of bacon across the glass.

Securing food to the rim can be a bit tricky, unless it's a cooked shrimp, because its natural curve is a perfect fit. Anything else you want to balance on the rim needs to be carefully slit partway through it. For wedges of lime and lemon, the peel creates a natural stopping point for the knife. Hold other foods securely on a cutting board and use a small and very sharp paring knife to slice only about one third of the way through the item.

Presentation Pointers

When you skewer a number of disparate elements for a mixed garnish, the size and shape of the pieces become important. Pick one item that is used in its entirety, like a cornichon or olive, and then trim the other items to size accordingly.

Small, thin items, such as fresh basil leaves or strips of prosciutto, should be folded and rolled.

Also take into account the effect that the moisture in one item might have on another. There's no way to make a marinated artichoke heart dry, but you should place it in between cubes of meats and cheeses rather than next to a cube of soft pretzel that could become soggy.

Basic Vegetables and Herbs

The aromatic celery stick became a classic because of its crunch, although many using people using a Bloody Mary medicinally for a hangover have been known to complain that the noise of chewing it sounds like a jackhammer inside their heads. But celery is hardly the only option.

Raw and Ready to Go

Choose from any of these foods and just prep them into the proper size pieces.

- Baby bok choy: Leave the pretty green leaves on and use a whole rib.

- Bell peppers: Red, green, yellow, orange, and purple can all be used. Cut them into strips to stick them into the drink, or use a wider section to stabilize garnishes resting on top of it.

- Carrots: They now come in more colors than orange. Look for yellow or purple "rainbow carrots" at your market. Cut them into long sticks.

- Cherry tomatoes: Alternate different colors on a skewer.

- Cucumbers: Buy English ones because they don't need peeling, and cut them into long sticks.

- Endive: Tuck the spears into the glass so the pretty pointed end is up.

- Fennel: Here's a use for the stalks that usually go to waste because you trim them off the bulb. Use stalks that have the feathery green fronds still attached.

- Herb sprigs: Fresh rosemary and sage are prime candidates because they have woody stems, and sprigs of fresh basil, parsley, and cilantro can be used if long enough. Chives are an especially nice choice in the spring when they have delicate purple flowers attached. Avoid sprigs of fresh thyme and marjoram because the stems are puny and won't sit up in the glass.

- Romaine lettuce: Use the small leaves from the hearts of the heads.

The Cooked Collection

I know that no one will die from eating a raw string bean or Brussels sprout, but they'd be much happier to eat these foods blanched so they are crisp-tender.

When blanching green vegetables, always have a bowl of ice water handy. Remove the vegetables from the boiling water with tongs, shaking them a bit to get as much water off as possible, and then plunge them into the ice water to stop the cooking.

How long to blanch the vegetables is a personal decision. I like my vegetables more tender than crisp, so I would leave them in the bubbling water for longer than those of you who want them basically raw but with a more pleasing color.

Here's a list of vegetables to be blanched.

- Asparagus spears
- Broccoli florets on a skewer
- Broccoli rabe ribs
- Brussels sprouts
- Cauliflower florets on a skewer
- Green beans or yellow wax beans
- Snow peas
- Sugar snap peas

Pickled Vegetables

It's almost destiny for fermented and cured vegetables to end up on tooth-picks and skewers sitting on top of a Bloody Mary. Any sort of pickle spear can be thrust into the glass, and small items can be joined together into an assemblage.

Here's a list of options.
- Artichoke hearts, cut into wedges
- Beets, cut into cubes or left whole if tiny
- Cherry peppers, plain or with a cube of cheese as a stuffing
- Cocktail onions
- Cornichons
- Giardiniera vegetables
- Okra
- Olives, any and all as long as they're pitted
- Pepperoncini

Sweet and Tangy Pickles

As Bloody Mary garnishes become more elaborate, spears of plain cucumber and sticks of celery are being replaced by pickled vegetables that add a flavor note to the drink as well as crunch. This sweet-and-sour pickle is one of my favorites because it plays well off the hot sauce in the drink.

Makes about 1 quart

1¼ pounds Kirby cucumbers
⅓ cup kosher salt or coarse sea salt
1 cup cider vinegar
⅔ cup firmly packed light brown sugar
1 tablespoon grated fresh ginger
1 tablespoon mustard seeds
1 tablespoon coriander seeds
1 teaspoon celery seeds

Trim the ends off the cucumbers and cut them into quarters or sixths lengthwise, depending on the diameter. Toss the cucumber spears with the salt in a large mixing bowl. Add 2 cups of ice cubes to the mixing bowl, and set aside for 2 hours, tossing the cucumbers occasionally as they soak. Drain the cucumber spears, rinse them well under cold running water, and then drain them again.

Combine the vinegar, sugar, ginger, mustard seeds, coriander seeds, and celery seeds with 1 cup of water in saucepan. Bring to a boil over medium-high heat, stirring occasionally. Add the cucumber spears to the pan, and bring the liquid back to a boil. Turn off the heat.

Transfer the vegetables and liquid to a clean storage container, and cool to room temperature. Refrigerate for at least 1 day before serving.

Notes: The pickles can be refrigerated for up to 5 days.

When cooking with any acid, like vinegar, citrus juices, or wine, you should never use an aluminum pan. The term you'll see in some recipes is "nonreactive." What this means is that it's made from stainless steel, enameled iron, or some other metal that will not give food a metallic taste.

Gingered Carrot Pickles

These carrots contain the intoxicating flavor of fresh ginger melded in a spicy, sweet-and-sour rice vinegar matrix. The carrots remain sturdy enough that they can be used to skewer other garnish foods, too.

Makes about 1 quart

1 pound thick carrots
¼ cup julienne of fresh ginger
3 small jalapeño or serrano chiles, seeds and ribs removed, sliced
1½ cups unseasoned rice vinegar
⅓ cup firmly packed light brown sugar
½ teaspoon salt

Cut the carrots in half lengthwise, and then place a half with the flat side down on a cutting board. Cut each half into thirds lengthwise, and then cut the long batons into 6-inch sections. Set aside.

Combine the ginger, chiles, vinegar, sugar, and salt in a saucepan. Bring to a boil over medium heat, stirring occasionally to dissolve the sugar. Reduce the heat to low, and simmer for 5 minutes.

Add the carrots, and simmer for 6 to 8 minutes, or until the carrots are crisp-tender. Transfer the carrots and liquid to a clean storage container, and cool to room temperature. Serve chilled.

Notes: The carrots can be made up to 2 weeks in advance and refrigerated.

Be careful in the vinegar aisle when buying rice vinegar, as some varieties are already seasoned; they're frequently called sushi vinegar. For all your cooking needs you want unseasoned rice vinegar.

Asian Sesame Pickles

Any time you see Asian ingredients in one of these Bloody Mary recipes, this quick pickle is a sure bet to use as a garnish. The pickles are ready to use in a matter of minutes, and once removed from the marinade they're good for a few days.

Makes about 1 quart

2 English cucumbers
¾ cup distilled white vinegar
¼ cup firmly packed light brown sugar
¼ cup toasted sesame oil
2 scallions, white parts and 4 inches of green tops, finely chopped
2 tablespoons Thai fish sauce (nam pla)
1 teaspoon crushed red pepper flakes, or more to taste

Chill the cucumbers in the freezer for 10 minutes. Cut the cucumbers lengthwise into sixths, and then cut each long piece crosswise into 3 sections. Combine the vinegar, sugar, oil, scallions, fish sauce, and red pepper flakes in a heavy, resealable plastic bag and stir well to dissolve the sugar.

Add the cucumbers and marinate for a minimum of 20 minutes at room temperature or up to 2 hours refrigerated. Drain the pickles from the marinade and pack them into a clean glass or plastic storage container.

Note: The pickles can be refrigerated for up to 5 days.

Dilly Beans

Crispy, brightly flavored pickled green beans are a great garnish for a Bloody Mary, and can be used to spear and hold up other garnishes, too. This version is a classic, and if you want to make it fiery just add the crushed red pepper flakes to the brine.

Makes about 1 quart

1 cup distilled white vinegar

1 tablespoon pickling salt or 2 tablespoons kosher salt

3 garlic cloves, cut into quarters

2 tablespoons chopped fresh dill

1 tablespoon granulated sugar

1 to 1½ teaspoons crushed red pepper flakes (optional)

12 ounces fresh green beans

Notes: The beans can be refrigerated for up to 3 months.

Pickling salt, sometimes called canning salt or preserving salt, is pure sodium chloride without any anticaking agents or iodine added. In that sense it's the equivalent of kosher salt, but kosher salt has big fluffy flakes and pickling salt is ground even finer than table salt. You can certainly use kosher salt, but double the volume to make up for the difference in granulation.

Combine 1 cup of water with the vinegar, pickling salt, garlic, dill, sugar, and crushed red pepper flakes, if using. Bring the mixture to a boil, then reduce the heat and simmer for 1 minute. Allow the brine to cool to room temperature.

Rinse and trim the green beans. Bring a large pot of water to a boil over high heat and have a bowl of ice water handy. Add the beans to the boiling water and blanch them for 45 seconds. Drain the beans and plunge them into the ice water to stop the cooking. Once the beans have chilled, pack them into a clean 1-quart glass jar.

Transfer the garlic cloves to the jar with the beans using a slotted spoon and then pour the brine over the beans to fill the jar. Refrigerate the beans for at least 2 days before eating them.

Variation: Substitute very thin spears of fresh asparagus for the green beans.

Fruits

It goes without saying that lemon and lime reign supreme in this category. While cutting a whole fruit cut into six wedges and slitting each piece to sit on the rim of the glass is the most common presentation, thin, round slices cut into the center can be even more attractive and add height.

If the mix for a specific drink includes a sweet fruit, such as the mango in Tropical Tango (page 136) or the watermelon in Blushing Pink Adobe (page 126), then a skewer strung with cubes of that fruit are a natural addition. But be careful mixing sweet fruit with most spicy Bloody Mary mixtures.

Meats

Packing proteins onto the top of a Bloody Mary is one of the big garnishing trends today; in fact, there are a few companies that transform pepperoni into functioning straws. You can finish the drink and then munch down the straw.

Cubes of grilled sausage—anything from Italian sausage to Cajun andouille and any number of items ending in the letters *wurst*—can be served at room temperature so they can be assembled in advance, as can cocktail hot dogs. Other possibilities for cooked meats include strips of steak or pork tenderloin, baby back ribs or lamb ribs, and skewers of chicken teriyaki.

The charcuterie department at the market is a treasure trove of options. Look for all the Italian meats like salami, soppressata, and prosciutto, as well as Spanish serrano ham. French pâtés can be great as long as the texture is firm; a silky foie gras mousse would not work while cubes of a hearty country pâté would be fine.

Beef Jerky

Jerky's popularity is skyrocketing, and it makes a great Bloody Mary garnish for those craving a carnivore fix. It's really easy to make at home, too. See page 154 for another flavor of jerky, and cooking tips for homemade jerky.

Makes about 12 ounces

2 pounds top round, bottom round, or flank steak
½ cup apple juice
¼ cup balsamic vinegar
6 garlic cloves
½ small white onion, diced
2 chipotle chiles in adobo sauce
2 tablespoons Dijon mustard
2 tablespoons honey
2 tablespoons Thai fish sauce (nam pla)
½ teaspoon liquid smoke
1 tablespoon coarsely ground black pepper
1 tablespoon smoked Spanish paprika
2 teaspoons crushed red pepper flakes, or more to taste

Trim all visible fat from the beef. Place it on a sheet of plastic wrap in the freezer for 30 to 40 minutes, or until it is firm but not frozen.

Combine the apple juice, vinegar, garlic, onion, chiles, mustard, honey, fish sauce, liquid smoke, black pepper, paprika, and red pepper flakes in a blender or food processor. Purée until smooth. Scrape the mixture into a heavy, resealable plastic bag.

Remove the meat from the freezer and cut it against the grain into ⅛-inch-thick slices. Add the slices to the marinade and move the beef around to make sure it is coated evenly. Marinate the beef in the refrigerator for 8 to 12 hours.

Line the bottom of the oven with a double layer of heavy-duty aluminum foil, and set the oven racks into the top uppermost rungs.

Remove the meat from the marinade and discard the marinade. Place the slices directly on the oven racks, leaving ½ inch between the slices. Set the oven to 170°F, and place the handle of a wooden spoon in the door to keep it slightly ajar.

Dry the meat for 3 hours, then turn the slices with tongs and dry for an additional 3 to 4 hours, or until you can rip a slice in half easily. Remove the jerky from the oven and transfer the slices to wire racks for at least 6 hours. Transfer the slices to an airtight container.

Note: The jerky can be stored at a cool room temperature for up to 2 months.

The way that the home oven can most closely replicate the results of the dehydrator ovens used by the pros is if the slices of beef are placed right on the oven racks rather than on a wire rack on top of a baking sheet. Warnings: Scrub your oven racks both before and after cooking the jerky, and cover the bottom of the oven with a double layer of heavy-duty aluminum foil. Things are going to get messy.

VARIATION: ASIAN JERKY

Substitute this marinade for the one in the master recipe.

2 cups tamari
½ cup firmly packed light brown sugar
¼ cup grated fresh ginger
5 garlic cloves, pushed through a garlic press
2 tablespoons toasted sesame oil
1 teaspoon freshly ground black pepper
¼ cup sesame seeds

Sprinkle the jerky with the sesame seeds when you place it in the oven.

Making Bacon Even Better

A crispy strip of thick-cut bacon is the swizzle stick of this decade when it comes to garnishing a Bloody Mary. And by far the easiest way to cook it is in the oven.

Line a rimmed baking sheet (or two) with heavy-duty aluminum foil, and place a wire rack on top of the foil. Preheat the oven to 400°F and place the bacon on the middle racks of the oven. Bake it for eighteen to twenty-five minutes, depending on the thickness of the bacon. There's no need to turn the strips over because they're on the rack.

That's for basic bacon. But there's no reason to stop there when you can flavor your bacon to harmonize with the seasonings in your Bloody Mary. Most of these coatings contain something sweet—brown sugar, maple syrup, or honey. And as is true when applying sweet barbecue sauces to food on the grill, the glazing should be done at the end of the cooking time to prevent burning. Better bacon is antithetical to burned bacon.

To glaze your strips—the porcine equivalent to gilding the lily—bake them for fifteen to eighteen minutes, or until the fat has rendered and the slices are brown but not yet crisp. The first thing you want to do is pour off the precious bacon fat to save it for another use, and then pat the slices with paper towels because you won't be able to do either once the glaze is applied.

Return the bacon rack to the baking sheet and brush both sides of the strips with your glaze of choice using a pastry brush. Return the bacon to the oven for an additional five to eight minutes, brushing the tops of the strips with the glaze at least one more time. Remove the bacon from the oven and allow the strips to cool on the rack.

Here are a number of glaze options. All are for one pound of thick-sliced bacon.

Spicy Sesame: Combine 3 tablespoons sriracha sauce with 2 tablespoons honey and 1 tablespoon toasted sesame oil. Sprinkle the strips with sesame seeds when you brush them with the glaze.

Bourbon-Maple: Combine 2 tablespoons firmly packed dark brown sugar, 2 tablespoons maple syrup, 1 tablespoon bourbon, and ½ teaspoon ground cinnamon or apple pie spice. Microwave on high for 30 seconds, or until the sugar dissolves.

Peppered Balsamic: Combine ¼ cup balsamic vinegar, 2 tablespoons firmly packed light brown sugar, ¾ teaspoon coarsely ground black pepper, and ½ teaspoon Italian seasoning. Microwave on high for 30 seconds, or until the sugar dissolves.

Spice-Rubbed: Combine 2 tablespoons cider vinegar, 2 tablespoons firmly packed light brown sugar, 1 tablespoon granulated garlic, 1½ teaspoons cayenne pepper, and ½ teaspoon herbes de Provence. Microwave on high for 30 seconds, or until the sugar dissolves.

Cheeses

Cubes of any semihard cheese that does not crumble easily, such as Gruyère, most Cheddars, and Swiss cheese, can be served on skewers by itself or alternated with pieces of sausage and pickled vegetables. Soft cheeses like Brie and Burrata should be avoided, although small balls of fresh mozzarella hold their shape nicely. Also avoid all members of the blue cheese family because they fall apart.

You can also tie the flavor of the cheese to the drink; jalapeño Jack is a great choice for any drink that contains Latin American flavors while Manchego is good, especially alternated with serrano ham, for a Spanish theme.

Herbed Parmesan Crisps

It doesn't get much easier than these thins—called *frico* in Italian—which are basically just Parmesan cheese that becomes lacy and crisp as it bakes. They're about as addictive a snack as you'll find, but you have to be careful placing them as a garnish because they can't get wet or they will lose their crunch. Sandwich them between two sturdy garnishes.

Makes 3 dozen pieces

2 cups freshly grated Parmesan cheese
2 tablespoons all-purpose flour
2 teaspoons herbes de Provence

Preheat the oven to 375°F. Line 2 baking sheets with silicone baking mats or parchment paper.

Combine the cheese and flour in a mixing bowl. Place 1-tablespoon portions on the baking sheets, leaving 1½ inches between the mounds. Toss the cheese mixture in the bowl frequently to keep the flour evenly distributed. Press the mounds flat with your fingers or the back of a spatula. Sprinkle with the herbes de Provence.

Bake for 9 to 12 minutes, or until brown. Cool the crisps on the baking sheets for 2 minutes, then remove them with a slotted spatula to a wire rack to cool completely.

Note: The crisps keep at room temperature for up to a week in an airtight container.

Variation: Substitute Italian seasoning for the herbes de Provence.

Cheddar Crackers

Admittedly, reading crushed potato chips in an ingredient list is unusual, but they make for the crunchiest and most flavorful cheese crackers you'll ever taste. If serving as a garnish to your Bloody Mary, you'll have to balance the cracker on another horizontal element like a pickle or celery stick.

Makes 2 dozen

5½ ounces potato chips
1½ cups grated sharp Cheddar cheese
5 tablespoons unsalted butter, melted
¼ cup all-purpose flour
½ teaspoon cayenne pepper, or more to taste

Preheat the oven to 350°F, and line a baking sheet with heavy-duty aluminum foil.

Place the potato chips in a food processor and chop them coarsely using on-and-off pulsing. Scrape the potato chip crumbs into a bowl and add the cheese, butter, flour, and cayenne. Stir until the mixture is combined and holds together when pressed in the palm of your hand.

Form 1 tablespoon of the mixture into a ball. Place it on the baking sheet and flatten it into a circle with the bottom of a floured glass or with your fingers. Repeat with the remaining dough, leaving 1 inch between the circles.

Bake the crackers for 15 to 18 minutes, or until browned. Cool the crackers on the baking sheet for 2 minutes, then transfer them with a spatula to a wire rack to cool completely. Serve at room temperature.

Notes: The crackers can be made 3 days in advance and kept at room temperature in an airtight container.

If you're grating cheese by hand, rather than with a food processor, coat the grater with vegetable oil spray and it will be much easier to clean.

Fish and Shellfish

Seafood is always an elegant garnish and there are so many species that are perfect to sit on the rim of a glass or on a skewer. Steamed or boiled shrimp or crab claws look really dramatic.

Smoked fish brings out all the salty flavors in the drink. Fish like smoked salmon can be cut into thin strips and then rolled into a flower shape to top a skewer, and anchovies are found already rolled into coils right in the cans. Don't use fish like smoked trout or smoked whitefish because the flesh has a tendency to break apart.

MOLLUSK MADNESS

While it takes some careful balancing, you can turn the top of your Bloody Mary into a raw bar. Make the drink in a Collins glass (because the diameter is fairly narrow) and then place a celery rib all the way down to the bottom. Across from the celery rib slide two lemon or lime wedges onto the rim, and then nestle a raw oyster or clam so it's leaning on top of the lemons and securely wedged into the celery.

Ceviche

Many of the Bloody Marys in Chapter 4 are made with Latin American ingredients like tomatillos and chiles, and skewers of ceviche make a dramatic as well as delicious garnish. Ceviche, pronounced *say-VEE-chay*, is the national dish of Peru and is also popular in Chile and other coastal areas of South America. While the fish remains raw it is acidulated so it appears to be cooked.

Makes enough for 12 garnishes

1 pound fresh, skinless thick white-fleshed fish
    fillets, such as snapper, halibut, or cod
1½ cups freshly squeezed lime juice
1 large shallot, minced
3 garlic cloves, minced
1 to 2 jalapeño or serrano chiles, seeds and ribs
    removed, finely chopped
¼ cup chopped fresh cilantro
3 tablespoons freshly squeezed orange juice
1 tablespoon olive oil
Salt and freshly ground black pepper
⅔ cup pitted green olives

Cut the fish into ¾-inch cubes and place them in a glass or stainless-steel mixing bowl along with the lime juice, shallot, and garlic. Stir well, and marinate the fish for 4 hours, or until a cube of fish looks cooked and is no longer translucent when broken apart.

Drain the fish in a colander, and return it to the mixing bowl. Stir in the chiles, cilantro, orange juice, and oil, and season with salt and black pepper to taste. Refrigerate for at least 30 minutes, and up to 6 hours. To serve, spear a few fish cubes onto one end of a bamboo skewer alternating with a few olives, and insert it into the Bloody Mary so that the cubes are visible.

Note: It's important to drain the fish from the lime juice after 4 hours or it will become too acidic.

Variation: Substitute sea scallops, cut in half or into quarters depending on their size, for the fish.

Just for Fun

This could also be called the miscellaneous garnish category. I love cubes of soft pretzels woven onto skewers, and cubes of flavorful focaccia can be balanced on the rim of the glass as well as threaded. Crispy snacks like pita crisps, bagel chips, melba toast, and chicharrónes are best if placed on top of sturdy foods like strips of bacon or wedges of bell peppers.

And for any drink that incorporates Asian ingredients always keep in mind that skewered pieces of sushi work well as long as they're rolled in nori.

Index

Note: Page references in *italics* indicate photographs.